Sensory Parenting
The Elementary Years

SCHOOL YEARS ARE EASIER WHEN YOUR CHILD'S SENSES ARE HAPPY!

Jackie Linder Olson
and
Britt Collins, MS, OTR

Sensory World
A proud imprint of Future Horizons

Sensory Parenting: The Elementary Years

All marketing and publishing rights guaranteed to and reserved by:

1010 N Davis Drive

Arlington, Texas 76012

(877) 775-8968

(682) 558-8941

(682) 558-8945 (fax)

E-mail: *info@sensoryworld.com*

www.sensoryworld.com

ISBN: 978-1935567417

Dedication

For Odin with love

~J.L.O.

For my friends and family

~B.C.

Acknowledgments

We'd like to thank our experts, who contributed so much to our book: Marla Roth-Fisch; Roianne Ahn, PhD; Susan Diamond, MA, CCC; Kay Toomey, PhD; Aviva Weiss, MA, OTR/L; Stephen Castor; Abbie Logwood; Khymberleigh Herweill-Levin; Lindsay Fogerty, MS, OTR; Lucy Jane Miller, PhD, OTR; and Alma Short.

Thank you to Wayne Gilpin, Jennifer Yacio, Heather Babiar, Shelley Hines, and everyone else at Sensory World that puts so much dedication into making our books the best they can be.

SENSORY PARENTING: THE ELEMENTARY YEARS

TABLE OF CONTENTS

SENSORY PARENTING: THE ELEMENTARY YEARS

Introduction

Many, if not most of us, have at least some sensory sensitivity that affects our ability to function in everyday life. One research study reports that one in 20 children today has Sensory Processing Disorder (SPD).[1] Another study indicates that one in six children experiences sensory symptoms that may affect his or her ability to function if everyday life.[2] Even though we offer in-depth information about SPD and related sensory issues in this book, we've really written it for all parents and all kids. Why? Because each of us has a unique set of sensory experiences and preferences that shapes the way we experience our world.

If you have already read our previous book, *Sensory Parenting: Newborns to Toddlers*, then this first section may be a little review for you. But, remember—repetition is the key to learning!

Let's begin by reviewing the eight sensory systems and how they can affect your child. Then, we will take you through the developmental stages of your child's elementary years. We'll go over red flags to look for to help you recognize your child's sensory sensitivities. We will also provide you with ideas on how to alleviate his or her sensory and behavioral issues. Finally, we will help guide you through the process of finding an appropriate therapist or other resource to help you with any worries you may have. You will also find information about how to work through a 504 plan or an Individualized Education Program (IEP) if your child needs it, and more.

Many of you are becoming "sensory savvy" and are learning all about the eight sensory systems and how these systems affect each of us differently. As they say, knowledge is power, and your child will reap the benefits of your efforts—as will the rest of your family.

According to the SPD Foundation, SPD is a condition that exists when sensory signals don't get organized into appropriate responses in the brain. When you process various types of sensory information, your brain takes in the sensory experience, organizes it, and then interprets what it means. If your brain has difficulty interpreting this sensory information, it can be what A. Jean Ayres, PhD, called a "neurological traffic jam." This means that certain parts of the brain are hindered from receiving the information needed to interpret sensory information correctly. For example, think about if someone you know well were to walk past you and touch you on the shoulder gently. Your brain would take this information and recognize that it is okay and that you don't have to be scared or worried. If someone you don't know were to walk past you and touch you on the shoulder, however, your brain might perceive this as a threat—or at least heighten your awareness to why a stranger is touching you. For most people, this process is automatic. For many children and adults who have sensory issues, however, an atypical response is produced.

In this book, Jackie's voice will come from a parent's perspective, and Britt's will be that of a pediatric occupational therapist. But, we will both use "I" or "we" when writing. We want this book to be a great resource tool for you as parents and caregivers, but we also want it to be a great reading adventure. We don't claim to know all of the answers, but we hope to bring more insight into your parenting skills than you had prior to reading the book. We also want to address the exciting milestones, as well as stages like the transition to starting preschool, moving up into the world of kindergarten, and all the various hiccups that come with attending elementary school. We will talk about making friends, having playdates, learning to read and write, playing sports, trying to fit in with peers, and more.

What exactly is *Sensory Parenting*? We came up with this term because we need to be aware of our sensory systems and the importance of nurturing them—especially as a parent. Our sensory systems do not have an "off" switch, so we never get a break from receiving sensory input. All day and night, our sensory systems send us signals, and our brains process that information. Just like parenting! Once your child is born, you are his parent from the word "go," and—again—there is no "off" switch. In short, *Sensory Parenting* means parenting with your child's sensory systems in mind.

For example, if your child has an auditory processing issue, he may not be able to fall asleep if the volume on your TV is too loud. This isn't something he will "grow out of." So, you'll need to adjust your lifestyle and parenting style to suit his sensory needs. Or, perhaps your child has a tactile aversion. As a sensory-friendly parent, you could work with your child on feeling different textures, exposing him to new tactile media in a safe and positive way, and finding adaptations to help him be able to tolerate tactile input. What do "adaptations" mean? Well, perhaps it means your child can wear rubber gloves while doing an art project. Then, you can ease him out of the gloves over time. Or, maybe it means allowing him to wear his jacket in the house if it makes him feel more snug. The sky is the limit when it comes to helping your child feel more comfortable in his own skin. Once you become a sensory-friendly parent, it's amazing what you'll come up with that works for your child.

Sensory Parenting also means taking care of your own sensory needs. Often, when parents start taking notice of their child's sensory systems, they become aware of their own, too. We may not notice, for example, as we get into our daily grind and move around on autopilot that our vision has been getting blurry over time. Maybe that's why you've been having chronic headaches! Perhaps your clothes feel too tight, or everything can seem really loud and overwhelming at times. The whole family suffers when we get too busy to take care of ourselves.

This book will give you lots of different options when it comes to choosing sensory therapies and activities. We will also explore sensory games your child can play. So, let's get started. And thanks for reading!

SENSORY PARENTING: THE ELEMENTARY YEARS

CHAPTER ONE

The Great *Sensory Parent* Detective

Wouldn't it be great if our kids were each born with an instruction manual, complete with a "broken parts" section? How easy would it be, if we could just "trouble shoot" and find a quick fix? If only we could turn to the page on tantrums and learn how to reset our child's systems. But, as you know, it's not that easy. Instead, what we can do is talk about how your child's sensory systems work. We can point out what to look for and how to decipher the signs that something that isn't working correctly. Maybe your child's sensory systems are not communicating properly with her brain. But, how do you recognize the signs, if you're not a trained therapist or doctor? We're here to help you learn how.

It's important for you as a parent to understand the vital role you play in your child's development and, if necessary, your child's sensory therapy. You spend more time with your child than anyone else, and you can learn how to be an integral part of your child's sensory well-being.

Keeping Records

One thing we have found through experience is that it's important to document your child's milestones, progress, and even setbacks. Many parents make a binder or folder that enables them to keep all of their child's medical information in one place. In addition to tracking your child's doctors' appointments, we recommend tracking any major events that occur in your child's life. Have you gotten a divorce recently? Has your child started a new school? Did you have a baby? Did the family pet pass away? Landmark events often create chaos and change in our children's lives. For a child with sensory issues, changes like these can induce havoc.

If you are checking your child for food allergies or trying out a new diet or lifestyle, then keeping records will be helpful for both you and your doctors. If it seems like little Jacob gets a tummy ache after eating pasta, make a note! Again, you're the parent detective, and it's easier to find patterns when you make notes to yourself about what's happening in the moment.

We know it can be hard to keep track of everything, and you may find yourself getting frustrated at having to keep records. But, we'd like to encourage you to try. If you have a child with special needs, it is unreal how many times you will have to reference this material. Personally, I have been overwhelmed by having to fill out all the forms for insurance, regional centers, and schools. Just when you think you're done, it's time to redo your child's triennial Individualized Education Program (IEP), and you're transported back to the land of filling-out-a-gazillion-forms. These records have saved me and given my aging memory a much-needed break.

Last, but not least, please remember to write down the positive things that occur in your child's life. Did your child say three words together? Did she have a successful playdate? Was she able to eat all of her broccoli? It's good to note what is working for your child, especially when it comes to finding the best therapists and making plans to help your child progress and stay on the right track.

Quick Sensory Checklist

We have compiled some clues your child may be giving you about how his or her sensory systems are functioning. While our sensory systems are complex, and there may be more going on than meets the eye, here's a starting point that could lead you in the right direction.

Fill out this checklist over time, after observing your child in his or her everyday environment. See if your child exhibits a particular behavior while playing in the park, or maybe while watching TV. Don't try to go after particular results, as this checklist is about what your child does naturally.

Once the checklist is completed, if you feel there is a concern in a certain sensory domain, please take the checklist with you when you talk to your pediatrician or therapist. Ideally, this is a reference to put you all on the same page and start a dialogue about what is going on with your child.

Yes	No	***THE EYES AND SIGHT***
❏	❏	Is your child able to track a moving target with her eyes, without moving her head?
❏	❏	Is your child able to stack blocks?
❏	❏	If age appropriate, is your child able to read?
❏	❏	Does your child complain about having headaches?
❏	❏	Does your child tilt her head sideways to look at objects or place them close to her eyes to see them better?

Yes	No	***THE EARS AND HEARING***
❏	❏	Does your child cover her ears with her hands to drown out noises?
❏	❏	Does your child talk or cry loudly over noise?
❏	❏	Does your child speak clearly?
❏	❏	Does your child tend to hear every little sound, even when others don't?

Yes	No	***THE NOSE AND SMELL***
❏	❏	Is your child sensitive to odors?
❏	❏	Is your child's nose congested often?
❏	❏	Does your child like or enjoy the taste of food?
❏	❏	Does your child constantly want to smell things?

Yes	No	***THE SKIN AND TOUCH***
❏	❏	Is dressing your child a nightmare?
❏	❏	Does your child not like to be messy?
❏	❏	Is your child fearful of physical contact with others?
❏	❏	Does your child want to touch others constantly?

Yes	No	***THE MOUTH, ORAL-MOTOR SKILLS, AND EATING***
❏	❏	Do certain food textures cause your child to gag or vomit?
❏	❏	Does your child refuse to try new foods?
❏	❏	Does your child have difficulty chewing or swallowing foods?

Yes	No	***THE VESTIBULAR SENSE AND BALANCE***
❑	❑	Is your child able to walk in a straight line?
❑	❑	Is your child afraid of heights or jumping?
❑	❑	Does your child have frequent motion sickness?
❑	❑	Does your child crave movement constantly?

Yes	No	***PROPRIOCEPTION AND BODY AWARENESS***
❑	❑	Does your child crave contact and rough play?
❑	❑	Does your child run into furniture or spill drinks often?
❑	❑	Does your child avoid playing on playground equipment?
❑	❑	Does your child trip and fall often?

Yes	No	***INTEROCEPTION AND INTERNAL SYSTEMS***
❑	❑	Does your child often complain about the weather?
❑	❑	Does your child not seem to understand whether water from a faucet is too hot or too cold?
❑	❑	Does your child not know when to stop eating?
❑	❑	Is your child always hungry?
❑	❑	Does your child have potty accidents after the age of 3 years?

Notes:

_____

_____

_____

_____

_____

_____

Please add other behaviors or concerns to the checklist that you wish to explore further with your child's doctor and/or therapist. Again, you are the "parent detective." Don't be afraid to write things down and seek answers to help your child.

The Eight Sensory Systems

Most of us are familiar with the five sensory systems of sight, sound, taste, smell, and touch. What we would like to do is break down these sensory systems "myth-buster" style. The more you know about the basics, the more you can help your child. We will also explore three more sensory systems, known as the vestibular, proprioceptive, and interoceptive systems. While these are big words, we promise they are easy to learn.

The Visual System and Sight

True or False: If your child has 20/20 eyesight, then he or she will not have vision problems.

The answer is "False." *Eyesight* is the ability to see, whereas *vision* refers to the way your child *processes* what he sees. There are many more factors involved in eyesight and vision than just being able to view letters and numbers on a chart. What happens to that information after the eyes receive it? To be able to "see" properly, it must not only travel to the brain unimpeded, but the brain must be able to translate those signals appropriately.

According to Ann M. Hoopes and Stanley A. Appelbaum, OD, FCOVD, authors of *Eye Power,* an eye doctor should examine your child's eye-muscle coordination, eye control, visual tracking, peripheral vision, visual perception, and visual information processing. They also suggest testing eye-hand and eye-body coordination and visualization, which is sometimes referred to as "seeing with the mind's eye."[3]

There are a few ways to tell if your child is having vision problems. Does he have difficulty tracking? Is it hard for him to copy letters or numbers off of the chalkboard at school? Does he seem to lose his place frequently when he reads? Does he tend to have poor depth perception? Does he get a headache while reading? Other clues might be if he's not able to read words, if he sees words "floating," or if the letters he sees are blurry.

In addition to or instead of wearing corrective lenses, some optometrists will prescribe vision exercises. While a doctor may give you some exercises to practice with your child, we recommend that any vision therapy be performed under the direction of a developmental optometrist or occupational therapist (OT). When it comes to the eyes, it is especially important to make sure you are working on the right things for your child's specific needs.

The Auditory System and Sound

True or False: The characteristics of a teacher's voice may determine how much knowledge a child will absorb.

Surprisingly, this is true. A teacher's voice is crucially important, as it supplies not only knowledge, but also the very energy that permits that knowledge to sink in and be recorded.[4] If a teacher presents information to his or her students in a more energetic voice, the students will leave the classroom with a higher energy level at the end of the day. The same is true if the teacher's voice is lethargic, stoic, or "low energy."

A child can pass a hearing test and still have an auditory processing concern. Just because your child can hear a bell or a tone, this does not mean she can process the language she hears. If a child is having an auditory issue that has gone undetected until the first or second grade, it may be that the child has relied on her visual and tactile senses to compensate. It's easier to look at pictures in a book and get the meaning of a story in preschool and kindergarten, but when the pictures are taken away and the teacher delivers an auditory lesson, auditory deficiencies start to pop out.

Some children cover their ears when things are too loud. Others may hear every little noise and get distracted by sounds frequently. Some children may not be able to process exactly what they hear, and they miss things (like when the teacher gives instructions in class). Many

OTs can do an auditory panel screening to help determine whether your child has difficulty processing the sounds she hears. A full workup can be performed by an audiologist, who can diagnose auditory processing disorder if appropriate.

The Olfactory System and Smell

True or False: There are two pathways into the nose—one from the nostrils and one from the inside of the mouth.

The answer to this is "True," and, to take it one step further, according to *What the Nose Knows*, by Avery Gilbert, "The apparent location of a smell—inside or outside of our body—determines how we perceive it."[5] So, we may perceive smells differently depending on which route to the nose they take—such as through our mouth or through our nose. This is why taste and smell go hand in hand. It's also a fact that expectation and presentation affect the way we smell, because the brain is what governs our sense of smell. If we expect it to smell good, it most likely will! On the other hand, if we have a bad olfactory experience, it becomes more prominent in our memory.

The most significant function of smell is to signify danger, such as a gas leak, or to let us know when food has spoiled. It is very important that we enjoy the smells of food. This enables us to eat. Each of us has an acquired sense of smell, meaning that we prefer smells we've been raised on in our own particular culture.

Your child's moods can be affected if she is having an olfactory dysfunction, such as anosmia (complete smell loss) or hyposmia (a reduced ability to smell). These are long-term conditions that are mostly caused by infectious disease or head injury.[5] Some children are even born "smell blind," or they experience phantosmia, in which they smell scents that aren't really there. These conditions can also lead to altered moods.[5] The loss of smell is not only detrimental to eating, but it can cause depression.

In case you were wondering, women have stinkier gas than men do.[5] Sorry, ladies—it's just a scientific fact.

The Tactile System and Touch

True or False: Our skin makes up 1% of our body weight.
The answer to this is "False." The skin is our largest organ, and, that being the case, our skin makes up about 15% of our body weight. So if you weighed 100 pounds, 15 pounds of it would be skin! That skin has many jobs, and it's the first system to develop in utero. We learn many things through touch, like how our mothers feel against our skin when we are babies. We learn about when things are dangerous to touch or when things are soft and cuddly. As we grow, our skin continues to protect us from the outside world and sends us countless signals and information about ourselves and our environment. Because our skin is our largest organ and contains so many nerve endings, a dysfunction with the tactile sense can be very disruptive to a child's daily life.

Does your child shy away from touching sticky or gooey things? Is your child a picky eater, and does he like only certain textures? Is your child bothered by tags in his shirt, or does he only want to wear certain textures of clothing? Does your child also crave touch and constantly touch other people or objects to the point of annoyance?

The good news is, there are many ways to help a child's sense of touch get back on track. With the proper help, you can retrain your child how to process the signals that go from his skin to his brain. We go into great depth on this in chapter 9.

The Gustatory System and Taste

True or False: The five specific tastes received by the gustatory receptors are sweet, salty, spicy, savory, and sassy.

Much as we wish this were true, this statement is nevertheless "False." The true tastes we can sense are salty, sour, bitter, sweet, savory, and spicy. While there are sour candies that are yummy, the actual function of the gustatory system is to warn us about sour and bitter foods being bad and possibly harmful if ingested. This cautionary skill is different than experiencing preferred or nonpreferred tastes, in terms of which foods we "like" to eat and which ones we don't. With children, the texture of the food is also important, as is the smell and the presentation. The gustatory system does not work independently.

We know you might be concerned if your child can't get enough spicy foods or wants to suck on lemons to give his taste buds a jolt. Kids with these tendencies may even put nonfood items into their mouths to kick-start their taste buds. Or, maybe your child is the opposite and refuses most foods. White, starchy foods may be the only ones that he will swallow.

While some kids will grow to love more foods as they get older, others may need feeding therapy or therapy with a sensory-based approach. Sometimes strengthening your child's oral-motor skills and desensitizing his mouth can work wonders. See chapter 4 for more information.

The Vestibular System and Movement

True or False: If your child's sense of balance is off, it will affect his eyesight and posture.

This is true, true, true! It makes it very difficult for your child to stand upright if his vestibular system is impaired. It is also nearly impossible to see clearly if his balance is unsteady. The vestibular system is governed by the inner ear, so it's dependent on the movement of the inner ear fluid. The vestibular system responds to motion, changes in head position, and gravitational pull. It is a very important system because of its influence over muscle tone, balance and equilibrium, posture, coordination of the two sides of the body together, and coordination of eye movements with head movements.

Children with vestibular dysfunction may often get nauseous in the car, have a fear of elevators or heights, avoid playground equipment, be unable to jump with both feet off the ground, and put their heads on the ground to be able to focus on toys.

The Proprioceptive System and Body Awareness

True or False: The proprioceptive system is not affected by rapid growth or sudden weight loss.

This is false. When your child is having growth spurts, it may take a little time for his proprioceptive system to be able to gauge how far his longer arms can reach. Be prepared for some spillage at the table or some tripping over his new, larger shoes.

The best way to describe the proprioceptive system is that it allows us to know where our body parts are in space. While this is a rather vague description, the complexities of this system are many. But, for simplification purposes, this is its basic function, and understanding the way it works will help you be able to "read" your child.

An example we like to use regarding the proprioceptive system is driving a car. Imagine you're driving now. Your hands are on the steering wheel, and your foot is on the gas pedal. You're looking out the front window, and the traffic light up ahead changes colors, from green to yellow. Since you know that a red light is coming, you switch your foot from the gas pedal to the brake. You didn't have to look under your dashboard to watch your foot switch pedals, because you know where your foot is and can gauge where you'd like it to go. Think for a second how many times your foot moves from the gas pedal to the brake pedal in just one trip to the store—and you never even had to look at it! This is your proprioceptive system at work.

For some children, the proprioceptive system may have difficulty telling them where their body parts are. Maybe they can't write without looking at their hand, or they cannot kick a ball without watching their foot. A more pronounced example would be if a child couldn't navigate a classroom without bumping into other children's chairs and desks because of poor proprioception.

Another misconception is that the proprioceptive system relies on the skin for information. In fact, this system gathers information from the inner ear and the stretch receptors in the muscular system and the joints.

The Interoceptive System

True or False: If your child always has hunger pains, he may not be getting the correct signals to his brain that his body is full.

Unfortunately, this is true. The interoceptive system is primarily made up of the internal organs, which send signals to the brain. An interoceptive dysfunction may show up in the form of a child who is oversensitive to weather changes. Or, a child may complain about the heartbeat in his chest, which is something most of us remain largely unaware of throughout the day. A child who has interoceptive problems may not be getting the signals that he has to go to the bathroom. A child with this issue can have real problems with potty training, because if he can't feel the sensation that he has to eliminate, then he can't get to the bathroom in time.

This system also controls your child's appetite. Is your child always hungry, without becoming full? Or, maybe he's never hungry at all? If you suspect that your child's interoceptive system may be dysfunctional, working with an OT is a must and is crucial to increasing your child's quality of life.

How to Help Your Child

Researching ways to help your child is step one. Good for you for picking up this book! If only all parents were as progressive and took action to benefit their children. Truly, the worst thing you can do is nothing. If something seems a little off to you, or you possibly detect a developmental delay (perhaps you even notice a full-blown sensory dysfunction), then, please—don't ignore it.

Talk to Your Pediatrician

Make sure your pediatrician knows your concerns. Perhaps he or she will give you a referral to a specialist for further evaluation. Remember that your doctor only sees your child for checkups and when he is sick. If you are noticing behaviors or tendencies that concern you, be sure to bring up these concerns with your doctor. Make a list and be ready, because you will only get an allotted amount of time to speak up.

If your pediatrician is not concerned, while you may be relieved, this does not mean that your child does not have an issue. Not all pediatricians are schooled in sensory processing.

If you think your child has possible sensory issues or even Sensory Processing Disorder (SPD), then you need to ask your pediatrician to refer you to an OT that is qualified in therapy with a sensory-integration approach.

Occupational Therapy

When you get a referral from your doctor, find an OT that is preferably outpatient or clinic based and qualified in therapy with a sensory-integration approach. That therapist can give you a questionnaire to fill out to gather information about your child's sensory systems. There are several sensory forms that OTs use. The Sensory Processing

Measure, the Sensory Profile, sensory checklists, and more are being developed as we speak. In addition to gathering this information, the OT should perform clinical observation and even use other standardized assessments to measure visual-motor, fine-motor, gross-motor, and bilateral coordination skills. Sometimes, insurance companies look for standardized scores for a child to qualify for occupational therapy, but, many times, children can qualify for privately based occupational therapy on the basis of professional judgment, as long as medical necessity is established in the occupational therapy report.

When the OT designs a treatment plan for your child, he or she will look at what your child is sensitive to. In terms of SPD, is your child overresponsive or underresponsive or a sensory craver? Does he have difficulty with postural control, sensory discrimination, or dyspraxia? Dr Lucy Jane Miller of the SPD Foundation in Denver, Colorado, is one of the leading SPD researchers in the field. According to Dr Miller et al (Figure 1), "There are at least six subtypes of SPD, and many people have a combination of more than one. With eight sensory systems and six or more subtypes, there are over 8 factorial × 6 factorial or 29,030,400 possible combinations. No wonder children with SPD can look so different!"[6] This means that not only does almost every one of you who is reading this book have a sensory sensitivity, but also, your brain processes sensory input in a unique way. We all have different responses to sensory information. (Note: Even though we talk about "children" in the following definitions, adolescents and adults can experience any component of SPD, as well.)

Dr Miller poses the various subtypes of SPD as the following:

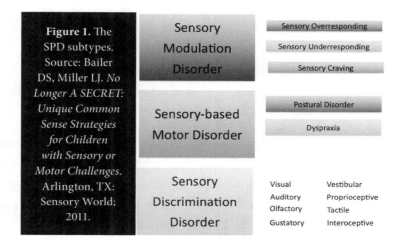

Figure 1. The SPD subtypes. Source: Bailer DS, Miller LJ. *No Longer A SECRET: Unique Common Sense Strategies for Children with Sensory or Motor Challenges.* Arlington, TX: Sensory World; 2011.

The first category of SPD is *sensory modulation disorder*, which is then broken down into three subtypes: sensory overresponsivity, sensory underresponsivity, and sensory craving.

Sensory overresponsivity occurs when the brain interprets sensory information as too intense, and the stimulation sends someone into a flight, fight, or freeze response. These individuals feel sensory stimulation too fast, and therefore they tend to avoid certain activities. They may cover their ears to shut out loud noises, resist movement, or withdraw from being touched. Here are ways in which some children may experience being sensory overresponsive in each sensory domain:

- **Vestibular:** The child does not engage in climbing, swinging, or spinning activities.
- **Tactile:** The child avoids touching sticky or gooey things.
- **Auditory:** The child may get extremely disorganized in noisy environments, like a mall or a sports arena.
- **Visual:** The child may feel uncomfortable in the sun, unless he wears sunglasses.
- **Olfactory:** The child runs from smells, such as the smell of dinner cooking.

- **Taste:** The child has only a small set of foods he will eat.
- **Proprioceptive:** The child may not like to feel pressure on his feet or legs and refuses to jump, hop, or skip.
- **Interoception:** The child may feel stomachaches frequently (and consequently visit the nurse's office often).

Sensory underresponsivity occurs when the brain is slow to interpret sensory information. Individuals with this type of SPD may appear withdrawn or self-absorbed, and they rarely initiate interactions with other people. They may demonstrate poor body awareness, owing to the underresponsiveness to tactile and deep-pressure input. This can make them look clumsy, slow, and lethargic. Children with underresponsivity may not notice when they get hurt or when the stove is too hot, because their touch system does not register information fast enough. Here are some ways that a child may experience being sensory underresponsive in each of the sensory domains:

- **Vestibular:** The child does not engage in physical activities and prefers sedentary tasks.
- **Tactile:** The child may not notice if he gets hurt or bumped.
- **Auditory:** The child doesn't respond to his name being called and may hum to himself while working on a task.
- **Visual:** The child loses his place when reading and complains of his eyes being tired.
- **Olfactory:** The child does not notice strong odors that others notice.
- **Taste:** The child does not notice or care if foods are spicy or bland.
- **Proprioceptive:** The child slumps in his chair or leans on walls. He may have weak muscles.
- **Interoception:** The child has potty accidents, is unaware of when he is hungry, and has poor body awareness.

Sensory craving occurs when a child craves certain sensory input over and over again. He wants to move constantly, crash into things, and jump. Some sensory cravers can be overly affectionate and get in others' space without realizing it. These children appear to be addicted to sensation and can't seem to get enough of it. Here are some ways that a child may experience being a sensory craver in each of the sensory systems:

- **Vestibular:** The child constantly craves the desire to spin, run, or move. He loves extreme, fast-moving activities, ice-skating, jumping off of high towers, riding roller coasters, and skateboarding fast.
- **Tactile:** The child wants to always touch other people or objects, put things in his mouth, or chew holes in his shirt.
- **Auditory:** The child constantly makes noises to himself, talks really loudly, and enjoys noisy environments.
- **Visual:** The child likes to watch things spin or move, more so than peers his age, and tends to like brightly colored objects.
- **Olfactory:** The child wants to smell everything he can, even non-food objects.
- **Taste:** The child craves strong flavors, like spicy, salty, and sour.
- **Proprioceptive:** The child constantly jumps, crashes, bumps into things, gives hard high-fives or hugs, and likes tightly fitting clothes.

The second category of SPD is *sensory-based motor disorder*, which is broken down into two subtypes: postural disorder and dyspraxia.

Children with postural disorder demonstrate poor core strength and decreased endurance. It is difficult for these children to stabilize their trunk and "co-contract" the muscles to help maintain their balance. Children who display weakness in this area tend to have difficulty performing efficient movements. They demonstrate poor body awareness, especially in the tactile and proprioceptive systems. They may exhibit a poor sitting or standing position, and their bodies have to work harder to maintain their posture, which can lead to fatigue.

Children who struggle with this area of difficulty may demonstrate a decreased ability to climb up a ladder or onto an uneven surface, like a swing. They tend to have to concentrate harder to maintain their core stability, so simple things like stepping onto an escalator or off the curb of the sidewalk are more difficult to execute.

Praxis is broken down into three parts: *(a)* coming up with an idea (ideation), *(b)* planning a sequence for the task, and *(c)* performing the motor task (motor planning). Children who have dyspraxia may have difficulty getting dressed, cutting out a shape, or coming up with new ideas for games to play with their peers. They may be accident prone, have poor ball-handling skills, or have difficulty with fine-motor skills. Sometimes, these children prefer sedentary activities or try to avoid motor tasks by "talking up" an idea or engaging in fantasy play, while never actually acting out the idea.

The third category of SPD is *sensory discrimination disorder,* which can affect any of the eight sensory systems. Being able to discriminate something means you can take in the information and attribute meaning to it. Children with sensory discrimination disorder have a "poor ability to interpret information or give meaning to the specific qualities of the stimuli."[7] They may have trouble telling the difference between a "*b*" and a "*d*." It may be difficult for them to reach into their pocket and be able to tell the difference between a paper clip and a penny without looking. Sometimes, it takes these children more time to process certain sensory stimuli.

What If My Child Has SPD?

We believe that almost all of us have some sensory sensitivity. However, when a certain issue starts to interfere with your child's ability to function, then it may become a disorder. It takes a highly skilled pediatrician, developmental pediatrician, psychologist, or OT to determine whether your child may have SPD. Either way, if your child is struggling with sensory issues or SPD, seek out a skilled OT who has been mentored and trained in SPD to get the best help for your child.

How Sensory Issues Can Affect You and Your Child

Have you wondered why your child melts down in the grocery store? It could be because you told her she could not have any cookies, but it could also be that the lights are too bright, the fresh fish smells too strong, and her sensory systems are not in sync. It could be that your child is overresponsive to the lights and smells in the store.

Take Sam, for instance. Sam loves to swing really high at the park. He swings so high, in fact, that it scares his mother, and she tries to get him to slow down. He cannot sit still in his seat in kindergarten, and he constantly touches the people around him. He enjoys jumping off the couch and crashing into a pile of pillows on the floor. His favorite pastime is wrestling with Dad. Sam is a sensory craver—he craves constant input to his body to be able to register the sensation.

Another example is Julie. Julie is 8 years old and is not very good at sports. She tries to play with her friends but is clumsy and awkward. She falls out of her chair at school a lot, and when she tries to climb the jungle gym at school, she doesn't seem to have the strength for it. Julie has poor postural stability and weak core muscles, which make many tasks difficult for her. Julie has postural disorder.

One morning, you wake up and your son Matt has dressed himself for school. His shirt is on backwards, his pants are all twisted, and he's wearing two different shoes. You laugh and help him get it all straightened out. When he gets to school, his teacher tells you that he has trouble writing his letters like all the other first graders. He cannot cut out even the simple shapes and doesn't seem to know how to play with the other boys on the playground. The teacher also has to zip up his jacket for him because he cannot do it. Matt is demonstrating dyspraxia and motor-planning problems.

Kristen is a good student at school and tries really hard. She also helps out a lot around the house with her younger siblings. You have always known that Kristen had some auditory processing issues, and sometimes you have to repeat yourself to make sure she understands you, but you also see that she is having trouble reading and writing at school. She sometimes pushes down so hard with her pencil that it breaks. When playing a new game, you discover that Kristen is not able to put her hand into the "feely box" and pull out the object that matches the picture. She cannot tell the difference between a car and an army figure by feel alone. Kristen appears to be having trouble with sensory discrimination.

How to Talk to Your Children about SPD

We asked one of our favorite authors about how she first talked to her son about SPD, and she gave us some exceptional insights.

Q&A with Marla Roth-Fisch, Author of Sensitive Sam

Marla Roth-Fisch is the mother of two sensational children. She is on the board of directors for the SPD Foundation and a dedicated advocate for SPD. Her first children's book, *Sensitive Sam*, won the 2009 Book of the Year Award by *Creative Child Magazine*. *Parents Magazine* chose *Sensitive Sam* as one of their "Healthy Reads" in the May 2010 issue, and the book has been endorsed by numerous experts, including Dr Lucy Jane Miller and Carol Stock Kranowitz.

Q: *Marla, when did you first talk to your child about SPD, and how did you bring up the topic?*
A: After a comprehensive evaluation and assessment by an OT that

was recommended to us, our son received an official diagnosis of SPD at the age of 3. For us, it wasn't the appropriate time to tell him. We needed to broach the subject with him in a "sensitive" way, since his emotions, stress, and anxiety levels ran high. To be blunt, he worried—a lot! This is common with children who have sensory issues.

Also, at the age of 3, would he really understand SPD? (After all, my husband and I had trouble wrapping our heads around it.) And—would he care to understand? We searched every online outlet, library, and parent organization for answers to our questions. We wanted to educate ourselves prior to talking with our son, just as any concerned and confused parent would do.

Holding off on giving our son the "label" of SPD seemed the way to go at this tender age. We had concerns that he would think of himself as "bad." We knew that we would need to talk with him about SPD sooner rather than later, and we chose to be creative in our approach to telling him. At first, we didn't mention the diagnosis. We simply explained the importance of soothing his frustrations, and we talked about the "sensory diet" assigned to him by the OT. We discussed how we would put that treatment and/or fun play into action, and we reassured him that by doing so, he would be better able to cope with his sensory issues. We told him over and over again that he isn't bad—just different.

Q: What was your son's reaction to having SPD?
A: Around the age of 5, we finally told our son that he has SPD. He reacted with total shock, and I think also a sense of relief. He understood that all the therapy we had been doing was helping him. His meltdowns became less frequent and severe. Not only could we calm him more quickly and easily by using the sensory diet strategies, but he could settle himself into a more peaceful state.

We kept it simple to understand, so as not to overwhelm him. We mentioned that:

- Other children have SPD—he is not alone.
- We love him completely, and he is very special to us.
- It is our mission to do all we can to relieve him of his over-responsiveness, so he can live a very fulfilling life.
- We will teach him the personal tools he needs to handle tough sensory situations.

As we continued doing therapies, including eating, speech, and writing therapy, our son became more confident and happy!

Q: As a parent, how do you deal with your son's SPD?
A: Temple Grandin says, "Sensory issues are daily issues." I *think* before I *do*, every day!

If I know that a certain smell triggers nausea and leads to gagging, I warn my son about it ahead of time. If I know that a certain place is going to be noisy, such as a concert, I bring earplugs or tissues he can put in his ears to mute the sound a bit. If we need to dress up for an event, I'll make sure we wear comfortable clothes that he likes. If we will be traveling, I set an itinerary he can review prior to departure. Our intention is not to eliminate activities or events in our lives, but instead to ease into them.

I think it's important not to cause additional overload for your child. If you notice that your child had a rough day at school—and you can usually tell if he did—then refrain from nagging him about doing homework right away. You might let him play outside first, enjoy a tasty (and healthy) snack, and then concentrate on homework. Trust me—pushing him if he's not ready will get you nowhere.

Q: Do you have sensory concerns of your own?
A: Yes, of course. Thirty years ago, there wasn't as much research or treatment available for SPD like there is now. I recall complaining

to my mom that I couldn't handle the sound of my own voice. She took me to see an ear, nose, and throat doctor, who had me lie down while he shot water into each one of my ears. Don't ask me why. To this day, I remember spinning and spinning in place because it made me feel better. I couldn't understand why the doctor wasn't able to help me. I think that was the extent of getting things checked out. Luckily, I was able to function each day, and I guess I "adapted" to my sensory challenges.

There are advantages of having SPD:

- Having a keen sense of smell allows me to alert my husband if something in the kitchen is beginning to burn (yes, it happens).
- I can hear the trash truck rolling in from miles away (a good reminder if we forgot to put out the trash). Also, I can always find spoiled food before the really horrible stench kicks in.
- I feel empathy toward others that have sensory challenges. I'm willing to do all I can to help, and that's why I'm dedicated to the SPD Foundation and their mission. You can visit *www.SPD Foundation.net* for more research, facts, and resources about SPD.

Q: What advice do you have for other parents of children with SPD?
A: If you notice possible signs and symptoms of SPD in your child, discuss them with your pediatrician and your child's teacher(s). You might even take the next step of getting an official diagnosis from an experienced OT. I always recommend keeping a journal of your child's actions and reactions that seem out of the "norm." Documentation will help you explain things to professionals better. You may end up seeing a pattern of challenging behaviors and their triggers. You could also share my book, *Sensitive Sam*, with your child, because it may help your child relate to someone else with SPD and let him know that he is not alone. The book also

helps adults understand what their child is experiencing, especially if the child isn't verbal.

If more than a few of the following symptoms fit your child, refer to the complete SPD Checklist on the SPD Foundation Web site.

Your infant or toddler:
— Has problems eating or sleeping
— Refuses to go to anyone but you
— Is irritable when being dressed; is uncomfortable in clothes
— Rarely plays with toys
— Resists cuddling, arches away when held
— Cannot self-calm
— Has a floppy or stiff body and/or motor delays

Your preschooler:
— Is overresponsive to touch, noises, smells, and/or other people
— Has difficulty making friends
— Has difficulty dressing, eating, sleeping, and/or toilet training
— Is clumsy and/or weak; has poor motor skills
— Is in constant motion or in everyone else's face and space
— Has frequent or long temper tantrums

Your grade schooler:
— Is overresponsive to touch, noises, smells, and/or other people
— Is easily distracted, fidgety, and/or aggressive; craves movement
— Is overwhelmed easily
— Has difficulty with handwriting or motor activities
— Has difficulty making friends
— Is unaware of pain and/or other people

Your adolescent or adult child:
— Is overresponsive to touch, noises, smells, and/or other people

___ Has poor self-esteem; is afraid of failing at new tasks
___ Is lethargic and slow
___ Is always on the go; is impulsive and/or distractible
___ Leaves tasks uncompleted
___ Is clumsy or slow; has poor motor skills or handwriting
___ Has difficulty staying focused on tasks
___ Has difficulty staying focused at work and in meetings

SENSORY PARENTING: THE ELEMENTARY YEARS

CHAPTER TWO

Developmental Milestones

Four Years of Age

There's no way around it—the first time your child goes to preschool or pre-kindergarten, it can be overwhelming for you as a parent. Have you left your child with sitters or in day care before? Does your child separate from you well, or has he been at home with you most of the time? If this is your first time transitioning your child into a classroom setting, it can be an emotional experience. Some children transition beautifully and are excited to go to school—and it's actually Mom who cries when she pulls out of the parking lot alone. Other times, it's the child who may cry or cling when he first gets used to going to preschool or pre-kindergarten.

Every child develops at a different rate. The following are just some guidelines to look for by the time your child reaches 4 years of age, whether your child goes to preschool or stays at home with you. If your child is significantly behind in any of the areas listed, ask your pediatrician or your child's teacher if you should be concerned.

By 4 years of age, your child should be able to:

Gross-Motor Skills and Movement
- Hop and stand on one foot for 5-10 seconds
- Go up and down stairs without support
- Kick a ball forward
- Throw a ball overhand
- Catch a bounced ball most of the time
- Do a somersault
- Climb up ladders
- Gallop

Fine-Motor/Hand Skills
- Copy a circle, a cross, and square shapes
- Draw a person with two to four body parts
- Use scissors by using two hands
- Copy some capital letters
- Dress and undress without assistance, with the exception of tying shoes and buttoning
- Use a fork and spoon to feed himself
- Cut on a line with scissors

Language
- Understand the concepts of "same" and "different"
- Master some basic rules of grammar (such as using plurals and past tense)
- Speak in sentences of five to six words

- Speak clearly enough for strangers to understand
- Follow three-step directions without cues
- Participate in rhyming games
- Use "What if" and "I hope" statements
- Say direct requests, like "Stop that" or "You're hurting me"
- Answer "when" questions
- Ask "why" questions

Cognitive Skills
- Want to know how the world works
- Recognize and name four colors
- Begin to count objects and recognize numbers
- Recall parts of a story
- Think literally
- Approach problems from a single point of view
- Begin to understand the concept of time
- Engage in fantasy play

Social and Emotional Skills
- Become more independent
- Be interested in new experiences
- Play "Mom" and "Dad"
- Cooperate with other children
- Increasingly engage in inventive fantasy play
- Prefer to play with other children over playing alone
- Want to please friends
- View himself as a whole person, involving body, mind, and feelings
- Confuse fantasy with reality
- Agree to rules, more often than not
- Be demanding about how he wants things done; realize he has an opinion
- Enjoy doing new things

- Be more and more creative with make-believe play
- Talk about what he likes and what he is interested in
- Become aware of his (or her) gender
- Take turns, share, and cooperate

Make note if your child demonstrates any of the following potential "red flags" by 4 years of age:

- Exhibits extremely fearful or timid behavior
- Exhibits extremely aggressive behavior
- Is unable to separate from you without major protest
- Shows little interest in playing with other children
- Refuses to respond to people in general or responds only superficially
- Seems unusually passive
- Rarely uses fantasy or imitation in play
- Seems unhappy or sad much of the time
- Doesn't engage in a variety of activities
- Avoids others or seems aloof with other children and adults
- Cannot understand two-part commands with prepositions ("Put the cup on the table" or "Get the ball under the couch")
- Doesn't know his first and last name
- Doesn't use plurals or past tense properly when speaking
- Doesn't talk about his daily activities and experiences
- Has trouble getting undressed
- Can't jump in place
- Has trouble scribbling
- Shows no interest in make believe or interactive games

Five Years of Age

By the time your child is 5, he is probably getting ready to start kinder-garten. Again, this can be a difficult transition for parents, but children are usually excited to be at school with their friends.

By 5 years of age, your child should be able to:

Gross-Motor Skills and Movement
- Skip
- Walk on a balance beam
- Demonstrate improved eye-hand coordination
- Catch a ball and throw a ball at a target
- Learn to jump rope
- Demonstrate more coordinated running ability

Fine-Motor/Hand Skills
- Draw a person with up to six body parts
- Copy a triangle and other geometric patterns
- Print the letters in his name
- Draw a person with a body
- Begin to demonstrate hand preference
- Color within the lines
- Cut out simple shapes

Language
- Tell stories with complete sentences
- Use a 1,500-word vocabulary
- Use plurals and verb tenses correctly
- Use future tense
- Ask the meanings of words
- Ask questions for informational purposes
- Begin to engage in cooperative play, such as making group decisions, assigning roles, and playing fairly

- Understand story sequences
- Repeat four digits when recited slowly
- Attend to a short story and answer questions about it

Cognitive Skills

- Seek out knowledge
- Understand the concept of "opposites"
- Begin to understand categories
- Show more independence in self-care skills
- Sometimes confuse fantasy with reality
- Count 10 or more objects
- Identify first, middle, and last

Social and Emotional Skills

- Begin to use conflict resolution with peers
- Want to participate with peers and have playdates
- Mimic adults and seek praise
- Distinguish right from wrong but not always recognize intent
- Have gender awareness
- Be demanding, but other times very cooperative
- Care for own toileting needs
- Be fearful of imaginary creatures

Make note if your child demonstrates any of the following potential "red flags" by 5 years of age:

- Cannot build a tower of six to eight blocks
- Is easily distracted and unable to concentrate on any single activity for more than 5 minutes
- Is unusually withdrawn
- Doesn't express a wide range of emotions
- Doesn't play a variety of games and activities
- Is unable to say his first and last name

- Doesn't draw pictures
- Loses skills he had previously
- Cannot wash and dry his hands
- Is unable to hold a crayon or pencil to draw or write
- Has trouble eating, sleeping, or using the toilet

Six and 7 Years of Age

Now your child has begun to gain experience in the world and has been in school for 1-2 years (unless you home-school). She is learning about her independence and how to interact better with her peers. The demands of school also begin to increase.

By 6 to 7 years of age, your child should be able to:

Gross-Motor Skills and Movement
- Ride a bicycle
- Demonstrate a higher level of coordination overall
- Tie her shoes
- Demonstrate improved ball-handling skills
- Demonstrate improved play skills overall
- Enjoy physical activities
- Swing, climb, and jump
- Play team sports, if desired

Fine-Motor/Hand Skills
- Button and zip
- Demonstrate hand dominance
- Sometimes still reverse letters and numbers (but this should decrease by the first grade)
- Write sentences and formulate complete thoughts when writing

Language
- Develop reasoning skills
- Move toward abstract thinking (conceptualize or generalize, understand that a concept can have multiple meanings)
- Read aloud with ease
- Sound out words when trying to spell or read them
- Create rhyming words
- Express ideas through writing
- Use an expressive vocabulary of 2,600-7,000 words
- Repeat a nine-word sentence

Cognitive Skills
- Demonstrate an increased attention span
- Become more independent
- Demonstrate difficulties with winning and losing games
- Become a more fluent reader
- Tell you what she is going to do
- Clean her room and make her own bed
- Begin fixing a simple meal independently (like pouring a bowl of cereal)
- Help out around the house
- Solve problems
- Demonstrate improved reading and math abilities
- Enjoy planning her day and having structure
- Demonstrate an increasingly vivid imagination
- Demonstrate an improved memory
- Understand same/different and opposites

Social and Emotional Skills
- Begin to separate from you more easily
- Enjoy playing with her peers, but sometimes want to be the boss
- Have peer conflicts sometimes

- Test her independence
- Separate from you more
- Want to have sleepovers with friends or spend the weekend with grandparents
- Start to think about the future
- Become aware of body image
- Make connections between feelings, thoughts, and actions
- Enjoy responsibility
- Form close friendships

Make note if your child demonstrates any of the following potential "red flags" by 6 to 7 years of age:

- Can't differentiate between fantasy and reality
- Has trouble making friends at school
- Is behind in any fine- or gross-motor skill
- Has trouble reading or writing
- Trips and falls a lot
- Is sensitive to certain movements, sounds, and sensations
- Seems unusually passive
- Is aggressive toward others

Eight to 11 Years of Age

Children develop at different rates, so it's harder to separate out their developmental milestones between 8 and 11 years of age. However, we have listed some general guidelines for this age group.

By 8 to 9 years of age, your child should be able to:

Motor and Movement Skills
- Participate in individual or team sports and activities
- Demonstrate increased fine-motor abilities

Cognitive Skills

- Read with confidence
- Gain a sense of responsibility
- Face more academic challenges
- Begin to see others' points of view

Social and Emotional Skills

- Understand social roles
- Demonstrate an increased desire for competition
- Learn to control emotions
- Develop healthy friendships and an awareness of the demands of peer pressure
- Become more aware of his or her body as puberty approaches

By 10 to 11 years of age, your child may:

- Experience a growth spurt with significant weight gain, muscle growth, and genital maturation (growth spurts begin earlier in girls but last longer in boys, who end up taller)
- Tolerate frustration better
- Demonstrate a good grasp of time
- Be able to plan and understand cause and effect
- Behave more rationally and logically
- Need affection and affirmation from adults
- Develop concrete thinking with a strong sense of fairness
- Begin to see conflicts between peers and the values of their parents
- Develop a handwriting style
- Demonstrate special gifts and talents
- Begin to think about future careers and occupations
- Shift her focus from play centered to academic
- Experience more peer pressure
- Become more independent from her family

- Become more aware of her body as puberty approaches
- Have feelings of insecurity and self-doubt
- Experience mood swings as she begins to move toward puberty

Make note if your child demonstrates any of the following potential "red flags" by 10 to 11 years of age:

- Doesn't deal well with losing
- Doesn't show empathy toward peers or animals
- Wants to spend all her time alone in her room and has no interest in making friends
- Says "no" to trying all new things
- Is not completely aware of rules and why some things are right and wrong
- Doesn't have control of her muscles to adjust speed, force, and direction for things such as dancing, playing basketball, and riding a bike
- Is not able to handle physical activity for more than a few minutes at a time; has no endurance for hiking or climbing

Again, we want to reiterate that every child develops at a different rate. If you feel that your child may not be where she needs to be, please check with your physician, her teacher, or even an OT or speech-language pathologist to find out whether you should be concerned with her delays.

Note: These checklists were adapted from several resources for developmental milestones, including the American Academy of Pediatrics and the Centers for Disease Control and Prevention. Other resources include the LinguiSystems "Guide to Communication Milestones," by Janet R. Lanza and Lunn K. Flahive, available at *Linguisystems.com*.

SENSORY PARENTING: THE ELEMENTARY YEARS

CHAPTER THREE

Engagement and Social Relationships

Engagement is such an important part of working with your child, but sometimes we don't realize how difficult it can be. Building positive relationships is also a crucial life skill that everyone needs to learn and understand. As a parent, when your baby was first born, all you did was engage with him and build a strong bond. You probably cuddled with him, smiled with him, made cooing noises, and held him in your arms while you looked into his eyes.

If you look back on when your child was an infant, was there a time when you thought it was hard to get his attention? Did you have a fussy baby, who was difficult to soothe? Did you possibly go through some postpartum depression and have trouble bonding with your child initially? This can be a very normal experience for mothers of a newborn.

As your child grew older, did you continue to have trouble engaging with him or feel like you had difficulty bonding? Many times, parents look back and realize that their child probably had several sensory sensitivities as an infant, but they never understood what they were at that time. Now you may be wondering, What did I do wrong? Well, we are here to tell you—nothing! You did not cause your child to have sensory sensitivities. Now that you are reading and learning more about your child's sensory systems, you can work with specialists to help you better understand your child's specific needs.

First and foremost, you have to be able to engage with your child. Meet him on his level, and get down on the floor and play with him. If you have a child who is 5 or 6 but appears to be delayed emotionally, you may still be playing games like "Peek-a-boo" or "tickle" types of games. You want to have your child look at you with a sparkle in his eye, and you want him to want to share an experience with Mom, Dad, grandparents, siblings, and friends. If a child is only focused in his own world and does not demonstrate the desire to share with others, this is a red flag.

Many children are so busy with school, after-school activities, sports, and—sometimes—therapy, that we forget how important it is to actually allow them to just "be kids" and play. You as a parent may be dealing with work, juggling your children's schedules, squeezing in your own personal workout, keeping up house, and trying to spend time with your significant other or even friends. It gets overwhelming to try and manage all of these things. You must take time out of your day to sit down and play with your child. For every hour of extra activities your child has, you should be spending an hour playing with him and engaging.

This does not mean sitting next to him, watching TV, or texting on your phone while he builds a Lego castle. This means actively engaging with your child. You are helping him learn to build social relationships. Children learn how to play with other children on the basis of how they play with you and their other caregivers. While it can be exhausting at times, it is very important to build this foundation for your child, so he can then go to school, make friends, and build relationships with others in his world.

Having a strong bond with your child is equally important. Of course there will be times when your children drive you crazy. Don't worry, one day you will drive them crazy too. This is all part of being a family and learning how to work together. When you have a good, trusting relationship with your child, it is much easier to challenge him to try something new or nonpreferred. If he trusts you, then he will be more likely to climb a little higher on the ladder at the playground or try the new vegetable that you cooked for dinner. If he is scared of falling asleep by himself, but you are there to comfort him and tell him you will be right in the next room, soothing him is a little easier when your relationship is strong.

As your children grow older and more independent, your relationship will change. As a mom, you might be the rule enforcer, and after a while your children get frustrated because they're tired of following the rules. As a dad, you may come home from work and wrestle around on the floor, and your kids love you. On the other hand, it may be that in your household, Dad is a little more strict with the rules, while it's Mom who's more laid back. No matter what, your relationship with your child will fluctuate, and there are going to be times when he says mean things, like "I hate you" or worse. But be patient, as your kids will also go through the normal emotional stages of life. Be supportive of their needs. Always let them know you are there for them, no matter what, and eventually they will realize how much you love and care for them.

Emotional Regulation

Emotional regulation is the process of managing and coping with emotion-related states on a moment-to-moment basis. Many children express emotional states by exhibiting behaviors that are related to their individual coping mechanisms.[8] Stanley Greenspan, MD, has done a lot of work on emotional and social functioning. He has written many books around this model and theory and has created the functional emotional developmental approach.[9] This approach describes the critical emotional capacities that characterize development, and it encompasses all aspects of development, including motor, cognitive, sensory, and language functioning.[9] According to Dr. Greenspan,

> In this model, there are two critical features of emotional and social functioning. One of these features relates to vital structure—building emotional and social interactions. This includes, for example, the ability to regulate emotions, form pleasurable relationships, use emotional signals for communication, develop a sense of self and psychological boundaries, and construct meaning and purpose. A second feature of the model involves the content or themes of emotional life, for example, aggression, fears, pleasure, sexuality, and so forth.[9]

Emotional regulation is a crucial part of how we function in our daily lives. If we cannot regulate our emotions, then we may blurt out our thoughts at inappropriate times or threaten to hurt someone, even though we don't mean it (like getting upset because someone cut in front of us in line). As adults, we usually know and understand when it's appropriate to allow our emotions to get the best of us and when it's not. Research has shown that for children to have the most success in school, they need to be able to develop good social skills and good emotional regulation.[10]

It is important to learn how to regulate ourselves, and teaching your child to regulate himself will have a longer-lasting effect than if you have to continuously regulate him. Although most young children need help regulating themselves when stressful or difficult situations arise, eventually they learn how to deal with these situations on their own. We can teach our children how to take deep breaths and slow down their bodies. We can give them a hug or apply deep pressure on their shoulders to try and help calm them down. We can also teach them how to give themselves a hug or squeeze something they keep in their pocket if they feel their bodies becoming more anxious, frustrated, or stressed out. You have to find what works for your child, and a lot of this is trial and error.

You also need to learn to regulate your own emotions and be able to maintain a calm state. This is especially so when your child comes to you and tells you she is being made fun of on the playground or she can't get her work done in class because it's too loud and the teacher keeps making her stay in from recess to finish her assignments.

There are six clusters of social skills that children learn before the age of 4 (as adapted from Dr Greenspan's work):

- Attention and regulation from 0-3 months: The child is calm and has interest in sights, sounds, movement, and being touched.
- Engaging with the world from 2-7 months: The child increasingly displays expressions of intimacy and relatedness.
- Interaction and communication from 3-10 months: The child participates in a range of back-and-forth interactions that involve emotional expressions, sounds, and hand gestures.
- Shared problem-solving from 9-18 months: The child engages in many social and emotional interactions in a rhythmic pattern.
- Meaningful use of ideas from 18-48 months: The child begins to use meaningful words or phrases and interactive pretend play with caregivers and peers to convey emotions and ideas.

- Logical thinking and perspective taking from 3-4½ years: The child builds logical connections between meaningful ideas and can see another person's perspective.

Infants start with trying to figure out how to regulate their sensory systems. They rely on their parents to help co-regulate them when they are hungry, tired, wet, or in need of comfort. They begin to self-regulate between birth and 3 months of age, as they grow and learn. Infants become interested in their world through their senses. For example, if the lights are bright, they may close their eyes. If they are uncomfortable lying on their stomachs, they may roll over. Anytime there is a new stimulus or experience, the baby's arousal level will increase slightly, and she will demonstrate an adaptive response to the stimuli.

Additionally, as infants grow, they learn to form relationships. This begins around 2 to 5 months of age. They begin by forming relationships with objects, then an individual person, and then people. A baby begins to engage with an object and explore it through her senses. She may start by looking at it, touching it, and putting it in her mouth. Then, she begins to engage with a person. The early implications of engagement are building blocks that affect a child's ability to generate attachments and create relationships later in life. Attachment is such an important part of a child's development. Studies have shown that securely attached infants tend to have better adaptability, social skills, and cognitive functioning than those with weaker attachment.[9] This carries over into school-aged children and adolescents, as children who experienced good attachments as infants create stronger friendships and relationships with others when they get older.

The next phase of social development is two-way communication. A child receives information from someone, and then she responds. Two-way communication is like the opening and closing of a circle. This applies to verbal communication, nonverbal communication, and gesturing. Two-way communication typically happens between 4 and 9 months of age. Children should be driven to want to communicate their needs to someone, and when they begin to reach out, smile, talk, and make requests to someone else, they open themselves up for someone to communicate back with them. Once they realize this is an effective way of getting their needs met, they continue this more and more. If a child does not understand this type of two-way communication, she may form a negative method of communicating her needs. For example, she may throw a temper tantrum to get you to feed her instead of attempting a positive means of communicating.

Social problem-solving occurs around 9 to 18 months of age. There is a beginning, middle, and end to social problem-solving. This is the stage where children play games and begin to engage more with others. If a child wants something, she may walk over to the object—but perhaps she can't quite reach it (the beginning). She may walk over to her mom and get some help reaching the object (the middle). Then, she obtains the object from Mom (the end). She has just problem-solved how to obtain something she wants by using appropriate social skills to achieve her end goal.

A child also begins to learn which behaviors are acceptable for any particular situation and which are not. It is not acceptable for her to throw herself on the floor when she wants Mommy to get her a cup of juice, but it is appropriate for her to take Mommy to the refrigerator and ask or gesture for her to open the door and get the juice out.

According to Dr Greenspan's book, the basic emotional messages of life include safety versus danger, approval versus disapproval, and acceptance versus rejection. All of these emotions can be portrayed through facial expressions, gestures, and words.[9]

By 18 to 30 months, children begin pretend play. Pretend play can be either concrete or abstract. A child should be able to engage in pretend play with an object and then be able to change what he is pretending the object to be. For example, a child may pretend he is fighting off the bad guys with a "sword," and then he can switch to using that same "sword" to put a magic spell on a princess. When pretending, a child should be able to use an object as a representation of another object, even if the two don't seem the same. Kids will put a banana up to their ear to pretend it's a telephone or pretend that a shoe is a hat. Then a child learns "perspective taking," or recognizing the perspective of someone else. This level of social skill can be very difficult for some children. If a child laughs when his friend falls and hurts herself, he may not be at this level yet. He may think that if her body is fine, then she is fine. It takes time for him to actually be able to feel the emotions of someone else. If he begins to ask his friend, "Are you okay?" after she falls, then you know he is beginning to reach this level of social development.

If you sense that your child has not quite reached these levels of social development, but his cognitive skills may be highly developed or at least age appropriate, he may be delayed emotionally. Many children can have a high level of cognitive skills and good motor skills but be delayed emotionally. These kids need help building these levels of engagement so they can learn the rules of engagement and social development. Sometimes your friends might say, "Well you baby him too much" or "Your child is spoiled," when, really, you need to look at his level of emotional regulation, where he is in his social development, and if he is able to interact appropriately with his peers and others around him.

If you enrich your child's experience and try to focus on the challenging areas, you can really help your child begin to grow emotionally. You can focus on expanding your child's sensory experiences. For example, if he is nervous about being around a lot of other children at the park, you can slowly introduce him to being around multiple children at once.

You could also focus on increasing the emotional component, such as modeling for him when his friend is hurt. Teach him to ask if she is okay, instead of laughing at her for falling. You can ask him how he feels and see if he can empathize with his peer.

The following are some general guidelines for when children reach these stages of emotional development. If you are concerned about your child's emotional development, seek out an experienced therapist or psychologist who knows and understands the levels of social-skills development.

In terms of social development, here are some red flags to watch out for from the ages of 4 to 7:[9]

- Does your child make friends at school and outside of school?
- Is your child able to negotiate with another person for something he wants?
- Does he have a close relationship with you and/or his other parent(s)?
- Is your child able to discuss his feelings and why he feels that way?
- Does your child demonstrate impulse control?

Basically, we all want the same thing—for our kids to have friends and to feel like they are a part of something. Every parent dreads hearing that his or her child was made fun of at school or wasn't invited to the birthday party that the rest of the kids are going to. It's even worse when you see your own child being mean to another child. Sometimes peers can be crude and mean and hurt your child's feelings for no reason. It is in our nature as parents to want to stand up for our child, but you have to think about both sides of the coin. Problem-solve through the reasons why your child is having a hard time making friends. Does he get along with another friend one on one but doesn't do as well in a group? Is he a little awkward socially and not always sure about the right thing to say? Or the right time to say it? Do you notice that you have a hard time playing well with others, and maybe you need to go back to the basics? Maybe you need to play with your child and teach him the correct rules of engagement. It isn't okay to just walk up to someone we think is unattractive and tell her she is ugly.

Britt's Story

When I was about 5 years old, I was at my grandparents' house. My grandfather's cousin was visiting, and she had thick glasses and was not a very attractive woman. She looked at me and said, "You sure are pretty," and I replied back, "Well you sure are yucky." My family was so embarrassed for me. I evidently did not realize that it was inappropriate to say that to her. Luckily, my grandfather's cousin and I have bonded over that moment, and now that she is 93 years old, she is still one of my favorite family members. However, I have yet to live this incident down.

Q&A on Social Success with Dr Roianne Ahn

We interviewed Dr Roianne Ahn, a psychologist who is a trained Developmental, Individual Difference, Relationship-based (DIR) Floortime therapist according to Dr Greenspan's model. Dr Ahn is passionate about helping people with SPD achieve social success and is committed to sharing the tools they need to achieve it! Dr Ahn infuses the DIR relationship-based play model into every aspect of her work with children, teenagers, adults, and families. Whether she's providing consultation, testing, therapy, or coaching, she focuses on creating positive and joyful relationship experiences that support and facilitate long-term learning. Dr Ahn helps individuals and caregivers understand the neurobiology of SPD and how to help those with SPD learn, relate, and grow successfully.

Q: What does the development of emotional regulation mean for children aged 4 to 11?
A: I really think about it as physical arousal regulation. Can they

get excited and calm down? Can they have low energy and get themselves riled up? How well can they stay in the "just right" arousal state?

Britt Explains the "Just Right" Arousal State

It is important to help a child stay in that "just right" arousal state, without getting "too high" or "too low." Sometimes, a child's "just right" arousal state is a very small window, and even the tiniest trigger can set her off in the wrong direction. We have to work on widening that level of arousal so the child can tolerate more changes, transitions, and adjustments to her day without shutting down or having a tantrum. Think of it in colors. The "just right" arousal state is green. When a child shuts down or has low arousal, her arousal state turns blue, and when she has high arousal or throws a tantrum, she's in a "red" state. We want to keep ourselves and our children in the "green" state—but this can be difficult. It is okay for a child to be in the blue when she is tired or sick. It is okay for a child to be in the red a little, if she is overly excited about Grandma coming to visit or frustrated that a child pushed her on the playground. But, she cannot act on that red arousal state inappropriately, and this is where she needs to know how to calm her body down to bring her back into the green.

Q: *How do you encourage families to learn how to play with their children, Dr Ahn?*
A: The first thing I do is get the parents to understand the child's nervous system and to understand from an SPD framework what makes that child's body happy. What makes the body happy makes

the emotions happy. Play for a child is whatever makes the body happy. Adults play primarily through conversation. Parents need to understand what is going on with their child and be able to "read" their child's signals from an arousal framework, as opposed to seeing good behavior versus bad behavior. Then, they can pick out whatever activities are truly fun for the child to do. As a parent, you have to tune into what your child's body likes.

In terms of connecting with your child, some people connect through their bodies, but others connect through words. Everyone has a different neurology. If the parents' and child's connection styles match, then it's easier, because the parents and child will more readily connect and create joy between them. They get the "twinkle in the eye," which is the magic we are looking for. This can be harder to achieve if the parents and the child have different profiles. The parents have to understand what kinds of play allow the child to experience joy. The child has to experience joy in the presence of the parent play partner to really facilitate the child's brain to be open and receptive to enable powerful learning.

Whether you are trying to teach manners, politeness, or how to ask questions, your child is going to learn better, faster, and in a more complex way if he is happily engaged with his play partner—you.

Q: How do you know if a child is experiencing an emotional meltdown versus a sensory issue?
A: To know the difference, you can't ever really tell in the middle of it. When the child's body and brain have gotten into tantrum mode, it all looks the same. To really determine the difference is to see what happened *before* the meltdown—you must observe the child over time to see if there are any patterns. The difficulty is that sensory triggers are not obvious, and children can have delayed

responses. It could have been a sensory trigger 10 to 30 minutes before, and you may not know about it until you really know your child. The biggest thing to know is that right in the middle of the behavior, it doesn't matter whether it's one or the other. The best book to consult about this is *The Explosive Child*, by Ross Greene. The problem-solving process involves finding out in what context the child is having a meltdown. Is it sensory related? Or, is the child regulated and calm, and then all of a sudden the child explodes? This would not be sensory based. You have to ask yourself, what are the precursors to the meltdown?

Q: What are some typical concerns families have when they come to you?
A: Here are some of the primary ones:
- How can my child learn to play better with friends?
- How can my child better handle his frustrations when he gets angry?
- How can my child sleep better, eat better, and have better physical regulation?

In general, it is going to be easier to tease out the sensory piece in younger children, versus an older child. The older a child gets, the more tightly woven the emotional, physical, and cognitive components, and the more difficult it is to identify a true underlying sensory issue. In a child who demonstrates anxiety, depression, or low self-esteem, you really have to look at the multidimensional aspects of the child's behavior, and it gets more complicated as the child gets older. Talk therapy, counseling, or medication won't always help, because there is more to the behavior than just mental health need. Someone has to address the underlying sensory issue, as well as look into the possibility of counseling or medication for the anxiety, depression, and low self-esteem.

A younger child's emotional layers can be overlooked, and parents need help addressing the emotional piece. By the same token, parents of an older child need to understand the sensory piece that often gets overlooked.

Social Skills

It is so important for children to develop social skills. One of the most common concerns we hear from parents is that their child struggles with social skills. Your child learns to socialize from you, so you really have to focus on playing with your child and teaching her the rules of engagement and play.

To be able to have successful friendships later in life, children have to learn through experiences with you and early peers to understand what behavior is acceptable. You need to show your child the importance of having empathy and understanding for others, how to sometimes be the leader and sometimes be the follower, and how to take turns in activities and share toys. Many children who attend preschool and day care begin to learn these concepts as they interact with other children their age. But, at some point, every child will come home upset because Sarah wouldn't play with her on the playground, or John wouldn't share the ball during the soccer game. As a parent you will try to help your child, because you want her to have friends, but you may not always know "how" to help her.

Social-Skills Classes

Social-skills programs are a wonderful way to introduce children to the world of friendships and developing people skills. Typically developing children will benefit from these programs, as well as special-needs kids. Social-skills classes are not the same as etiquette classes, where the focus is on manners and which fork to use at the dinner table. In social-skills class, the focus is on how to interact in real-life situations, and manners are often addressed, as well. It is vital that all children learn how to engage with others, even if it is just to ask a police officer for help or to ask for directions to a grocery store. Social skills and life skills go hand in hand. Arm your child with the skills that will help her through her schooling, career, and relationships.

There are a few different types of social-skills classes available. They can include a group of children, either a small bunch or a classroom full. Sometimes classes are conducted one on one, until the child is ready for a group class. These courses can occur at school, privately, or even at a community center. Figure out what is best for your child, as you know your child's social-skills abilities better than anyone.

If your child struggles with social interactions, it may be best to find an older peer that is patient and willing to tolerate some of your child's inabilities in understanding the rules of play. You can build up your child's self-esteem with successful playdates with this older child and then see about having her play with a child closer to her age. When structuring your child's playdate, have something prepared for your child and her friend to do. Start with baking, doing a craft project, or building an obstacle course. This gives you the opportunity to watch how your child interacts with her peer and vice versa. It also helps you be able to give your child subtle social cues when needed. Then, if things are going well, you can back away a little and let the kids play on their own. But, stay close by in case your child or the peer needs you to help with any situation that may arise.

Ideally, social-skills classes should include both boys and girls, since your child will realistically need to be able to interact with both, whether at school, within the family, or at places of work. It's best if your child knows how to approach both sexes and is able to interact with both naturally. It's okay to do playdates and activities with all boys or all girls, but you don't want your child to be segregated to the point of not being able to engage with a mixed group.

It's okay if your child gravitates to one buddy and is not as interested in the other kids. Yes, it's best to include everyone, but you can't force people to like each other if they don't. Use this as a time to teach your child to tolerate others and be kind to the kids that she may not prefer to play with.

And finally, you want to make sure that the people who are leading the social-skills group are experienced in working with children with a variety of needs, including sensory issues. The classes should be fun! If learning about social skills occurs in an entertaining environment, your child will be motivated to learn. It doesn't have to be a circus, but you can't just sit kids in a circle without any direction. We suggest making sure that the social-skills group is structured and has a plan in place. In the case of sensory issues, the instructors need to be aware if your child becomes withdrawn because it's too loud, as she may be sensitive to too much noise. Or, if your child becomes slightly aggressive or upset, it may be due to the fact that she doesn't like being touched by others.

It is important for the kids in the group to do a gross-motor movement activity that can help them learn how to take turns, wait their turn, share ideas, and engage with the other children. Then you can do an activity or game that will help the children work on winning and losing, playing together as a team, and sharing. Sometimes it's nice to have a snack as a group, so children learn how to socialize while they eat. They may need help knowing how to start a conversation or how to ask their friend a question but also listen to their answer. Sometimes visual cues can be helpful, as can practicing beforehand. Role-playing with your child, so she knows what to expect in social situations, can be very beneficial.

Many children are more comfortable engaging with adults than with other kids. Make sure your child engages with her peers and does not focus only on the social-skills teacher.

If your child has anxiety, make sure you address it, and let your so-cial-skills instructor know your concerns. Instructors of these classes are usually great at helping your child feel safe and secure so she can work on building successful relationships.

If your child graduates and matures out of social-skills classes, it's always good to continue the social-skills process. Perhaps it's time for group vocal lessons or karate—whatever your child is interested in—as long as it requires social interaction. Would your son be interested in an etiquette class, where he learns how to ask a girl to dance? Let your child build robots in his room if he wants, but don't allow him to have so much time alone that he doesn't know how to interact with and con-tribute to society.

Supervised Playdates

If your child is extremely shy or has behavioral issues, you may want to start with supervised playdates. This is when an OT, speech-language pathologist, social worker, or aide takes your child and one other child on an outing. This can happen at home, at the park, or as a planned event, such as bowling or a movie. As an example, let's say an OT facilitates the playdate. The OT will help you pick an appropriate peer that will help set your child up for success. Maybe it's a neighbor or someone from your church group, a cousin, or even a sibling, if a sibling is the only one available. Try to make it someone that your child is comfortable with.

Once a peer is selected, set a playdate with a start and end time. This will help take some of the pressure off of your child if she has a hard time socializing, since she knows it will be over at a specified time. Organiza-tion is key on these playdates, so have an activity planned. For example, if you're meeting at the park, the OT may tell you to bring two board games, or maybe the OT will have some obstacle-course equipment for the children to go through together. Incorporating movement into these playdates is always a good idea.

During this supervised playdate, the OT will help your child engage with the other child. Perhaps she will give your child questions to ask the other child to start a conversation. The OT will also help curb inappropriate behaviors by redirecting and encouraging desired social behaviors. If you have an IEP, supervised playdates may come with specific goals for your child to work on during this time.

If you invite a peer over to play with your child, make sure you start with a structured activity, so you can help your child start off on the right foot. It could be baking cookies or making an obstacle course in the living room. Then, you may see that the two kids are ready to have a little free play to build with Legos or play Barbies, which are both open-ended tasks. Watch how they interact with each other, and only interfere if you need to. Again, your child may need a visual schedule or pictures to help her remember the rules of engagement and how to react appropriately to her peer. It is difficult to know what to say or how to react when something your friend does upsets you or takes you by surprise. Allow your child to take breaks from the peer partner if needed during the playdate. Also make sure the peer is following the same rules of engagement that you are requiring your child to follow. You don't want to have a peer over that is mean or knocks down your kid's tower every time she builds it.

Small Buddy Group

Some social-skills groups have three or four children. This is enough for them to bounce off of each other and engage with more than one child, but not so overwhelming that your child shuts down like some children do in a larger group. An OT or social-skills leader will have activities for the children to do that require them to interact with one another. Maybe your child will learn not to pull hair if she gets angry with a child for taking her toy. The OTs and social-skills leaders are great at redirecting and, most importantly, arming your child with words and behaviors that are appropriate.

Society Doesn't Always Make Sense!

We live in a world where we speak in slang and have vernaculars that are particular to our fields of business and even where we are located geographically. Our tone and delivery can also change the meanings of words entirely. Sometimes, this is very difficult for our kiddos to pick up and manage, especially if they have special needs. As adults, we know what "What's up?" means. We automatically translate this question into, "What's going on with you?" To a child who thinks literally, however, this question refers to the direction "up," and he may answer, "The sky."

There are millions of unwritten societal rules, such as not standing too close to someone in line. Just imagine if a gentleman was pressing his chest into your back while you waited in line at the post office. It would be creepy, right? While this is not as disturbing when it happens in school, your child might get into trouble if he's pressing in on another child or gets into another child's space.

The general rules you want to teach your child include:

- Respecting body space (don't stand too close to others)
- Not contacting others inappropriately, especially violently
- Respecting others' ideas
- Sharing toys with others
- Taking turns
- Not staring at people
- Being mindful of what you say to others (you don't want to offend them)
- Saying "please" and "thank you" (always trying to be polite)
- Not interrupting others when talking

- Trying to listen to others' interests
- Watching others' facial expressions and being able to recognize if they are interested in your conversation or not

Reading Facial Expressions and Body Language

For many children who struggle with social interactions, sometimes the hardest part is being able to read other people's social cues. If you are trying to tell your buddy a really interesting story about trains, but he starts to look away and yawn, you may not realize that he is not as interested in your train story as you are. If someone is telling your child something and she grimaces or makes an unusual facial expression, your child may not understand how to read that or how to react. Sometimes when I work with kids in the clinic, they get their feelings hurt if I joke around with them, because they don't understand the humor in my voice. If I say, "You're a silly goose," they think that I'm making fun of them or calling them a name. I have one kiddo in particular who only wants me to call him "Nick"—not "Nicholas," or "buddy," or "dude." Just "Nick"! He lets me know if I forget and accidentally call him something else. Another child I work with thinks I am mad at him if I try to tell him something serious. If I explain to him about a safety rule of the gym, he cries and melts down because he thinks he is in trouble.

We have to be aware of our tone of voice, body language, and facial expressions and how they come across when we interact with a child that may be sensitive or may not quite grasp being able to read those cues.

One way to work on this is to identify and talk about individual emotions. Also, you can take pictures of your child when he demonstrates different facial expressions. Then, you can show him the photos so he can see what he looks like when he's happy, sad, or mad. There are many "emotion games" on the market today that may also help your child in this area.

Jackie's Experience with Social-Skills Groups

For myself and my son, social-skills groups have been something we've been immersed in since he was 3 years old. We started with a class at his special-needs school that split the children into groups of three at a time. This was life changing for us, because my son learned to use his words and to be able to tell kids "no" when they got in his space. I'm not sure he actually engaged with the other children at first, but he was "with" them, and it was a start. He had so much social anxiety in the beginning that he sat across the table from the other kids, as far away as he could get. But, at least he sat at the table with them for snack time. Progress came in baby steps. His social-skills teachers were extremely helpful and encouraging. I had to stay in the room with him at first, but the teachers slowly helped me depart once he was comfortable.

After 2 years, we moved to a new school and a new program. My son learned to function better in slightly bigger groups, with up to seven children on some days. While he detested noise and children coming toward him, he learned to interact with others, if only on a one-on-one basis. He also got to observe other kids, which was good and bad. It was great, in terms of the role models I wanted him to emulate. But it was also awful, because he was an imitator. If there was a hand flapper in the group, he came home flapping his arms.

When my son turned 6, he moved into a standard school program that didn't offer social-skills groups, so I had to search for other options. I found a lovely art teacher that also taught social skills, and we started classes immediately. She incorporated art with lessons and manners and encouraged the kids to communicate. We left the group when one child was disturbing my son too much, but we returned when the teacher started a new group. Sometimes you have to figure out what is best for your child, and just go with it.

Since we've had such success with social groups, I've also been involved in social-skills playdates with other children. It's been a beneficial way for my child to get that one-on-one time he needs, and he's a great model. We've met other kids and OTs in the park and gone on day trips to Disneyland, all in the name of social skills.

Now, we've also tried a few things that have not worked out for us—namely cooking class and magic class. These were complete disasters, because my son couldn't tolerate the environment. But, he's currently enjoying gymnastics. It's a beginning class for boys that he attends on Saturdays. The kids don't engage as much as I'd like, but my son does try. One thing that is still hard for him is how much the boys tease each other, because he's very literal and sensitive. But, he's learning and soaking it all in.

My advice to parents is to never give up on social-skills development. It's made all the difference for us, and I'm proud when my son walks into a new situation and is able to communicate. If only more typically developing children had these skills! It's not always easy to find a good fit, but the payoffs will last a lifetime—so be diligent. Don't put off developing social skills until your child is older. Start from the beginning… and keep it going.

Q&A with Susan Diamond, MA, CCC

Susan Diamond, MA, CCC, is a licensed speech-language pathologist with a private practice in Alameda, California. She provides diagnosis and treatment for communication disorders and specializes in social-language skills. Sue enjoys more than 25 years of experience in the field and is the author of three books, including *Social Rules for Kids: The Top 100 Social Rules Kids Need to Succeed*. She has appeared on TV as a social-skills expert and conducts workshops for parents, therapists, and teachers. Her passion is helping people communicate successfully.

Q: At what age do you think kids should start developing social skills?
A: Early intervention is always best. If a child displays social or emotional issues related to autism or other neurocognitive disorders, social-skills therapy is imperative. When a child does not develop social skills at the same rate as his peers, it is time for intervention. To determine the rate, we look at normal developmental milestones. For instance, at the age of 2 to 3 years, a child should look at someone who is talking, engage in simple make-believe play, and seek attention from others. If the child is not interacting at this level, then social-skills therapy is warranted. If a school-aged child does not have friends, then certainly the child is in need of social-skills help. The ages for starting social-skills therapy may vary, according to a child's individual needs. A child may experience difficulty in social situations for the first time in elementary or middle school, owing to an inability to keep up the rapid pace of speaking and processing. He may also lack an understanding of subtle nonverbal gestures, slang, and tone of voice. When a child is in need of social-skills help, this is the right time to begin.

Q: What kind of expectations are reasonable when participating in a social-skills class?
A: The social-skills professional will observe and assess a child's social-skills needs and then share his or her findings with the parents. Goals are set according to these needs. For example, if a child is not taking turns talking, the goal will be to take turns in a conversation (or a game, depending upon the child's age). The social-skills teacher may have the child engage in many turn-taking activities, like passing a ball back and forth. When the ball is passed, it is that child's turn to talk. Another activity may be to have a child describe an event, while his peers are cued to make comments and ask questions in a reciprocal flow. Parents can

expect updates on progress and suggested activities to do at home to generalize the skills. There are ample gains when these skills are practiced consistently. Overall, you should expect your child to experience progress in his social communication abilities and thus feel more at ease in social situations.

Q: *How often and how long should kids go to social-skills class?*
A: The length of time and frequency are determined by the child's individual needs. A child with autism may attend a social-skills class multiple times per week, owing to needed support in many areas of social communication. A child who needs to learn only a few skills may require fewer sessions. For instance, if a child is experiencing difficulty with multiple social skills, such as making eye contact, reading social cues, taking turns, and understanding nonverbal communication (like gestures and facial expressions), then the sessions will be longer and more frequent. A child who is working on just two of these skills may progress more quickly, thus requiring fewer classes. There are other factors involved, as well, such as the consistency of the skills being practiced, the child's motivation level, and whether the group is a good fit. The social-skills class should end when the child has made ample progress.

Q: *What do you think is the most important thing kids need to learn about social skills?*
A: I think the most important thing to teach a child regarding social skills is how to make and keep friends. Children want to interact, join in, play, and have friends. If they have issues with social skills, they may be isolated or ostracized by their peers. Peers may laugh when kids miss subtle social cues and respond inappropriately. Peers may also find it odd when kids ask questions or make comments that are off topic. To help children learn to make

and keep friends, we must teach them social skills directly. I have found that by using written social rules, children make progress.

For example, imagine a child who runs up to her friends at recess to play. She comes into the circle and stands too close. Her peers become uncomfortable, and the social group disperses, leaving her behind. When she practices the rule, "Don't be a space invader," which refers to personal space, she becomes successful in her stance the next time. Many children can navigate the playground at school and understand the subtle, implied rules. However, this can be difficult for children with social-skills issues. When they learn and practice social rules, they will learn how to make and keep friends.

Q: How can parents help teach their kids social skills?
A: Parents can use the following tips:

- Discuss a social situation before it occurs. Talk about interactions and what might be said. Encourage questions or concerns from your child. Problem-solve what can happen and how it can be handled. Role-play the scenario.
- Role-play greetings and joining in.
- Teach your child that when he asks someone else to play, another child may say "no." The other child may not be in the mood that day. Your child can say, "Okay," and walk away. He can find someone who wants to play and/or interact.
- Discuss what being a good friend means and talk about how your child's behaviors affect whether someone wants to be a friend.
- Structure playdates; decide ahead of time what activities may be played and how to take turns choosing activities. Make playdates fun for social success.
- Talk about how to respond when your child is being teased.

Your child can either ignore the teasing or answer back, "You wish," or "So?" Teach your child to not get upset.

- Talk about rumors. You may not know if a rumor is true. You may be tricked. Do not pass the rumor along. It can be hurtful.
- Talk about being a victim (someone who is teased often) and how to change the role by being strong and keeping the power.
- Talk about negotiating at school. When playing tag, if you are told to be "it" three times in a row, you can say, "I was 'it' last time. It is someone else's turn to be 'it.'"
- Role-play how to deliver a response with the right tone of voice and the right body language.
- Play "Charades" to help with body language. Watch TV with the sound off to observe, label, interpret, and imitate the actors' body language.
- Use mirrors to look at facial expressions. Say an emotion and make your face match the emotion.
- Make a scrapbook by using magazine pictures. Discuss the feelings depicted in the photos by talking about posture, gesturing, and facial expressions.

For more information on social rules for kids, visit Susan's Web site at *www.diamondlanguage.com.*

Highly Recommended Reading

Susan Diamond's book, *Social Rules for Kids: The Top 100 Social Rules Kids Need to Succeed,* is a comprehensive resource for both parents and elementary-aged children (even teens). It's organized perfectly, in an easy-to-read format that serves as a quick reference. Topics discussed include talking and listening, friends, school, bullying, feelings, body language, and manners. Each chapter is broken down into social rules, such as "Accept a friend's answers" and "Say no to a friend." This book allows parents to teach their children these rules in an applicable way that will help kids understand these previously unwritten rules.

Another outstanding book regarding social skills is *It's So Much Work to Be Your Friend: Helping the Child with Learning Disabilities Find Social Success*, by Richard Lavoie. This book is chock full of information, starting with why children with learning disorders are wired differently. Richard discusses anxiety and goes into great depth on practicing social skills at home, at school, and in the world.

SENSORY PARENTING: THE ELEMENTARY YEARS

CHAPTER FOUR

Sensory Needs at Home

A Sensory-Friendly Home

A sensory-friendly home is warm and inviting. It doesn't have to look like a Pottery Barn catalog, but it should be orderly and comfortable. Try to think of ways to make your home a sensory delight to be in. If there are any plumbing issues, have them fixed so the house doesn't smell. Don't clutter up your home with a bunch of stuff that convolutes the mind. If there is a construction project going on, like a kitchen remodel, come up with a timeline and a plan for how to keep your home sensory friendly throughout the duration of the project. A sensory-friendly home is one that is both safe and sanitary.

Try and keep the toxins in your home to a minimum, to alleviate stress when it comes to your child's sensory systems. Smoking is not only bad for you, but it's horrible for your children and your home. The smoke gets into everything, including the drapes and the furniture. We encourage you to use nontoxic cleaning products, so your child's brain (and nose) aren't affected by potent chemicals. Some children are sensitive to burning candles and smelly plug-ins. Does your dog always have gas? Maybe you can try switching his dog food until it gets slightly better.

Be mindful of the noises in and around your house. Is the TV always blaring? Are you situated below a flight pattern, with planes roaring overhead every hour? Do your upstairs neighbors walk with heavy footsteps? Take note if you or your children are irritable or are having a hard time sleeping because of noise. Make changes to accommodate your child, by introducing either white noise or calming music.

Think about your sensory memories while growing up. Was your Uncle Joe's TV tortuously loud? Did your grandma make aromatic cinnamon buns? Was the blue sitting room a soothing place to read? Mimic these sensory memories for your child or create new ones that you can all enjoy.

Waking Up, Going to Bed, and Everything in Between

The way we live our lives affects our sensory systems. If your child is not getting enough sleep, his sensory systems may suffer. If he's not eating healthy foods or getting enough movement and exercise, or not giving himself time to recharge, then he will be in sensory upheaval. All of these factors affect your child's internal state. This is what makes a healthy overall lifestyle for you, your child, and your child's sensory systems so important.

Good Mornings

For some kids, mornings are tough. Maybe it takes them a while to wake up, and maybe they wake up cranky. Sometimes, the way we wake up can determine the course of our entire day. Here are some tips to start your child's morning off right.

1. **Sunlight.** If possible, let the light shine through the windows to help your child wake up naturally.
2. **Movement.** While some kids like to "veg out" in front of the TV to wake up, it's better if they get their bodies moving, instead. As you begin to create a sensory lifestyle for your child, give him some activities to do in the morning to get his body moving. You could create an obstacle course, have him help cook breakfast, and allow him to earn stars or points on his chore chart in the morning as he helps with the daily routine. Jumping on a miniature trampoline is an excellent way for him to get out that early morning energy, and it will stimulate his vestibular and proprioceptive systems.
3. **Healthy food.** Kick-start your child in the morning by giving him nourishing foods to eat. A protein, like an egg or some peanut butter, with fruit is ideal. Froot Loops may be fortified with vitamins, but they're also packed with sugar. Choose a fuel that will give your child's body energy until snack time or recess. It is best if you provide your child with a protein, a fruit or vegetable, and a starch at every meal—and at least one of these should be one of your child's "preferred" foods. Help your child learn about new foods, even if he doesn't want to eat them initially.
4. **Proprioception.** Does your child function better after getting a big hug or some squeezes to his shoulders? Maybe he can wear his backpack prior to leaving the house, so he gets that sensory feedback he craves. (But make sure his backpack does not weigh more than 10% to 15% of his body weight!)

Daily Living Skills

Now that your child is in elementary school, it's time she became more independent. That said, she may still need some help in the hygiene department, especially if you want to make sure she gets an excellent review at the dentist.

Haircuts

Some children are sensitive to haircuts. While we're pretty certain that nobody's hair actually hurts when it's cut, we do understand that for some children, scissors are scary. It could also be that the salon is noisy and busy, and people are rushing in and out. The frock they drape over your child could be too tight on her neck or feel painful to the touch. Maybe the sound of the hairdryers hurts her ears. She could also have fear and anxiety about getting her hair cut: "Will it hurt?" "What if the hairdresser accidentally cuts me with the scissors?" "What if I look ugly?" "What if people at school laugh at my haircut?" It could be an entire whirlwind of things.

If your child is having concerns about having her hair cut, try to be patient with her. Talk about her fears or sensory needs, and maybe you can work it out together. Perhaps wearing an apron during the haircut would be better than having to wear the frock, if it bothers her. Maybe she could wear some ear buds and listen to her favorite tunes to relax. Would she feel better if you held her hand while she gets her hair cut? Sometimes Mom can make everything better. Try situating her so she's not looking in the mirror, so she can't necessarily see what is happening. Distract her with a movie or game, and reward her at the end with something special.

Booger Eaters

I know what it's like to have a booger eater. I'm not proud, and I've checked online so I know I'm not alone—but it's still important to teach your child about healthy nostril hygiene. I'm still trying with my son. At first, I thought it was a hand-to-mouth thing, like it can be for smokers, but then I ruled that out. I've read that nose-picking is natural and that we do it to clean our nostrils out—but the "eating" part is what kills me. Why do they do it, and how do we stop them from doing it? Britt assures me that this is natural and that kids will grow out of it. I'm still hoping she's right. If your child doesn't realize the social effects of eating his boogers, you may want to write a social story about it to help him understand what other kids might say about him.

Brushing Teeth

Brushing teeth can be a battle for many parents. Trying to hold your child down every morning is not a fun way to begin the day—it can start things off on the wrong foot. Wrestling over the toothbrush is also not a great way to calm your child down before bed. First things first— try various flavors of toothpaste, and maybe let your child pick one out. Don't get mad if he doesn't like it—the idea is to find one that he can tolerate. There are many fabulous toothbrushes to choose from. Again, let him pick out a toothbrush and maybe get one he can decorate himself. For youngsters with a sensitive mouth, you can try a vibrating toothbrush, and use it on both the inside and outside of the mouth to help desensitize the area while brushing.

Have your child explore the inside of his mouth with the toothbrush. Watch him brush, making sure he gets all of his teeth, and if not, then take a turn yourself. This may not make him happy, but if you promise extra reading time before bed or a special treat in his lunch box, he'll be more agreeable. Allow him to brush your teeth, so he feels empowered.

Take turns brushing. Even if you only use water to brush at first, it's better than nothing!

A good, old-fashioned teeth-brushing chart can help motivate kids with heightened sensitivity. Perhaps they can brush their way to a new game for their Nintendo DS.

Nail Trimming

Remember the days when you held your little baby and effortlessly clipped her nails while she slept? Those days are gone. If your child is sensitive to having her nails cut or cutting her own nails, do it when she gets out of the bath, as her nails will be softer. Maybe the best time to clip is when she's engrossed in her favorite television show—you might even be able to get both feet and hands at once. Some children won't mind getting a mani-pedi at the spa, or you can pretend to be at a salon at home. Be mindful of ticklish feet, as you don't want to get kicked. Try to pick a time when your child doesn't have too much pent-up energy.

Once your child starts clipping her nails herself, make sure she doesn't cut them too short, as that can be painful, too. Some children do better when they have control of the clippers. It may help them feel slightly less sensitive.

Baths (and Showers)

At some point in elementary school, your child is most likely going to take a bath or shower by herself. While we always hope she'll use soap and wash her hair with shampoo, most of bath time is spent playing with bath toys or daydreaming. Some kids do not like the bath for a number of reasons:

- They may not like the temperature change when they remove their clothes. Perhaps you could turn up the heat before bath time, so your child doesn't get as cold when she gets in and out of the tub.

- Maybe the sound of the water filling the tub disturbs your child. Perhaps you could run the bath (and add nontoxic bubble bath) before summoning her to the bathroom.
- If your child shows distress while tipping her head back to wash her hair, try giving her a washcloth to press against her eyes. This will keep the water from dripping down into her face and allow her to keep her head upright. She may not like the vestibular input she gets with her head tipped back.
- Is the bath painful? Ask your child if the water temperature is bothersome, or maybe it's the act of washing her hair that bothers her. You could stop using bubble bath, as it makes some children feel itchy and uncomfortable. If a true problem persists, meet with an OT about a potential tactile-defensive issue.

Sometimes, kids really do not like taking a bath, and for this we suggest trying a shower. Make sure the shower has a safe surface for her to stand on without slipping. It may be a new sensation for her at first, with the water coming down on her head, but encourage her to try to tolerate the water. Check the temperature and make sure the water pressure isn't blasting her skull.

Washing Hands

While even most adults don't wash their hands enough, we need to encourage children to wash their hands as much as possible, especially after going to the restroom and before eating. While kids are at school, they are subjected to countless germs and viruses. Washing hands can help keep them healthy.

If they don't like washing their hands, find out if it's a water temperature issue. Does the water faucet at school only put out icy cold water? Does the soap make her hands smell funny or itch? Maybe she could try a hand sanitizer and keep it at her desk. Or, you could teach her to rub her hands together to warm them up and then wash them quickly. Are her hands chapped from the cold weather? Maybe you can put some petroleum jelly or Aquaphor ointment on her hands while she sleeps. Or, maybe she has blisters on her hands from playing on the monkey bars at school. If this is the case, washing her hands is even more important while they heal. Work with your child to get the cleanest and healthiest hands possible.

Dressing

Some children have a hard time tolerating the sensation of textures against their skin, and for them, it is difficult to get dressed. It's okay to purchase loose-fitting clothes that will be more comfortable, but try to make them presentable and not sloppy. There are a lot of sensory-friendly clothing options these days.

A calming technique that you may want to try with your child before getting dressed is applying deep pressure to her shoulders, massaging her arms or shoulders, or rubbing a terrycloth washcloth on her arms and legs. Some children like getting hand massages with a scented lotion they find appealing. The length of time for these calming strategies is typically 3 to 5 minutes.

During elementary school, your child will learn how to dress himself. We're not talking about fashion, here—we mean skills like zipping, buttoning, snapping, tying, pulling clothes over his head, and maneuvering socks onto his feet. If your child is having problems with these tasks, maybe he needs to work on his fine- and gross-motor skills. He may also have trouble with his motor-planning skills. This could make it difficult for him to sequence out the steps of dressing and figuring out how to balance and coordinate his body to step into his pant legs.

Teaching Dressing Skills

- When teaching your child to tie his shoes, it may be easier for him if you give him two different colors of laces. It makes tying them a cinch. Start with his foot out of the shoe first. Have him master tying the laces this way before he tries to tie them while wearing the shoe.
- Zipping and unzipping a sleeping bag is good practice with a zipper.
- Give him a visual schedule of the sequence for dressing to help him know what comes first, second, third, and so on.
- When you are not in a hurry, take the time to help your child practice getting dressed (like on a Saturday morning).

Long Afternoons and Weekends

People often find themselves watching TV all evening or all weekend. We get it—"America's Top Model" marathons can be addictive. However, with a little planning, you and your family can use this time for more sensory adventures. Maybe you can have a modeling challenge in your own backyard or your apartment courtyard. Grab a camera or use your cell phone camera to take some fun pictures of your kiddo, and then edit the photos with some funny effects on the computer. You can never have enough family photos. You could even make homemade scrapbooks out of them as a family!

It can be tough if you've worked all week and you haven't had time to plan anything. But, even an impromptu trip to the park can get both you and the kids outdoors. Sometimes, I like to act like a local tourist and see what is going on where we live. We've enjoyed a Chinese New Year festival, a rubber ducky race, and a pumpkin competition by checking online to see what's happening in our area. There are apps you can get for your phone that provide ideas, as well, such as the Roadside America app.

If you're really struggling to find something to do and your child needs some movement, review our lists of suggestions for good proprioceptive and vestibular activities in chapter 9. We offer many ideas that should keep your child busy and are good for him, too.

Safe Havens

Some youngsters need somewhere to get away and collect themselves. If they're overwhelmed or stressed, it would be great to have an area in which they can unwind. Perhaps it's just a quiet spot in the living room, with a beanbag and a cozy blanket. You could also put a tent up for your child to crawl inside, a cozy space with some pillows where he can relax and calm down. Maybe you have a guest bedroom upstairs that has a comfy chair to lounge in, where your child can read or listen to music softly. Do you have a place where the lights are slightly dimmed and the temperature is comfortable, where your child can regroup and take a break from whatever is stressing his sensory systems?

Having a go-to place to relax and shut out the world can be reenergizing and allow your child to better cope with the stress of the day. Maybe you can do some guided imagery with him and help him relax if he can't calm down. There are CDs available at *imageryforkids.com* that can help guide your child through mental relaxation and give him some tools to use when he is feeling stressed and anxious.

You can tell that your child needs some time to himself if he's gotten too manic or shuts down and seems overwhelmed. The safe haven is not a time-out or a punishment, and you should make this very clear to your child. We all need time to regroup.

Homework

Definitely allow your child to relax and wind down when he gets home from school, before asking a lot of questions or having him start his homework. This can be difficult, especially if there is another child in the house, or friends, or cousins who are able to come over right after school. Some kids may be able to sit down and finish their homework independently, without taking a break first. These little superheroes are the rare exception. Most of us parents struggle to get our children to do their homework during the week, and it can be even more challenging to get them to do homework on the weekends.

Establishing an after-school routine for your child can be very helpful. When he walks in the door, you might set the microwave or stove timer for 60 minutes. This is his time to desensitize and unwind from the day. He may want to do the same thing every day to get out of "overload mode," and that is okay. Again, think about yourself, when you come home—you have a routine, don't you? It is okay for children to need this, too. Transitioning back into the "home" routine is paramount after school. Provide a calm environment, with a relaxed pace when he walks in the door. Attempt to keep a routine going, and if a break in the routine is needed for a dentist appointment or soccer practice, help your child plan for it a few days in advance.

Be aware that homework can sometimes be the sole source of overload for a child. In our experience, school personnel often believe that quantity is more important than quality when it comes to homework assignments. However, Britt and I believe that traditional academic homework is highly overrated. We feel that your child works so hard at school all day, he should be able to get a break when he comes home. At least make sure your child has something fun or relaxing to do when he gets home from school before going straight back to schoolwork.

What we personally like to do is to encourage children to get their homework done at a comfortable pace. Make sure your child is allowed to take sensory breaks while he does his homework, to help keep him focused and attending to the task.

When your child starts his homework, you should try to read with him, practice his speech words or signs with him, assist with his math problems, and so on. Involve yourself in whatever your child is working on at school, so you can help your child generalize and carry over the skills he learns into his home life and his community. Opportunities for incorporating these skills into his day-to-day routine are all around you. For instance, give your child a grocery list when you go shopping, and have him help you keep track of the items you buy. When you drive to the dentist's office, let him help with giving directions and finding landmarks along the way. Have him read over the menu at a restaurant, hand the waitress money to pay the bill, and count the change.

Sleeping and Sleeping Environments

After an active day, it's time to calm down and go to sleep. This is not so easy for kids who have trouble shutting down their sensory systems. A routine is paramount for children in elementary school, especially. Sometimes they seem a bit older and we're tempted to let them stay up late, but it's really best to keep them on a schedule and give their bodies that much-needed sleep.

Your Child's Bed and Room Environment

Your child's bed should be comfy. Just like with Goldilocks and the three bears, a bed shouldn't be too hard or too soft. It should be just right. We recommend using nontoxic bedding, meaning it doesn't have chemicals in it—such as "wrinkle free" additives. If your child needs a weighted blanket, but he gets hot when he uses it, just know there are options for you at Fun and Function *(funandfunction.com)*. They have a weighted blanket with mesh holes in it, allowing air to circulate around his body.

Keep TVs and video games out of your child's bedroom, or he'll be tempted to stay up all night watching SpongeBob. The less temptation in his room, the better. We also prefer soothing rooms with little decoration. If you want a theme, that's fine, but forget the grand showroom and keep it mellow. Visual distractions are stimulating, and you want your child to feel relaxed when he's in his room (especially when it's time to go to sleep).

Tips for getting your kiddo off to dreamland:

- Have a routine. Brush teeth, read a bedtime story, give him some deep-pressure squeezes if he likes it, and then it's "lights out." Do whatever works best for you and your child.
- Kids just need time to wind down, so start your routine early! Maybe some calming music or deep-pressure squeezes would help.
- Lighting matters. Low LED lights are soothing for a child who doesn't want to sleep in a pitch-black room. Pick a mesmerizing night-light that switches colors to soothe your child to sleep.
- Set up a small waterfall or dehumidifier. Some children drift off to sleep to the sound of water, and others may benefit from having less moisture in the air. Either way, these machines can make consistent white noise that will gently "shush" your child to sleep.
- White-noise machines can be helpful for lulling your youngster to sleep. Make sure that the settings are calming and not stimulating for your child. I happen to know that if you put a recording of frogs croaking in my bedroom, I'd be up all night. But, many children benefit from the sounds of birds chirping or whales singing. Other children prefer the white noise of a fan that drowns out the sounds of televisions, traffic, telephone conversations, and movements in the house.

Q&A on Feeding Questions with Dr Kay Toomey

Dr Kay Toomey is a pediatric psychologist. For more than 20 years, she has worked with children who don't want to eat. She has developed the Sequential-Oral-Sensory (SOS) approach to feeding as a family-centered program for assessing and treating children with feeding problems. Dr Toomey speaks internationally about her approach. She also acts as a consultant to Gerber. She is currently the president of Toomey & Associates, Inc, as well as the clinical director of SOS Feeding Solutions at the STAR Center (the Sensory Therapy and Research Center) with Dr Lucy Jane Miller.

Q: *What are the red flags that indicate a child needs feeding therapy?*
A: Figure 2 indicates red flags that may warrant feeding therapy:

Red Flags

Is this child a candidate for referral? (Maybe, if any of the following are present)

__ Ongoing, poor weight gain (ie, percentile rates falling) or weight loss
__ Ongoing choking, gagging, or coughing during meals
__ Ongoing problems with vomiting
__ More than one incident of nasal reflux
__ History of a traumatic choking incident
__ History of eating and breathing coordination problems, with ongoing respiratory issues
__ Child reported to be "picky" at two or more child wellness checkups
__ Inability to transition to baby food purees by 10 months of age
__ Inability to accept any table-food solids by 12 months of age
__ Inability to transition from breast and/or bottle feeding to drinking from a cup by 16 months of age
__ Child not weaned off of baby foods by 16 months of age
__ Aversion or avoidance of all foods in a specific texture or nutrition group
__ Food range of less than 20 foods, especially if foods are being dropped over time, with no new foods replacing those that are lost
__ Crying and/or arching of the back occurring at most meals
__ Family fighting about food and feeding (ie, meals are battles)
__ Child repeatedly reported to be difficult for everyone to feed
__ Parental history of an eating disorder, with a child not meeting weight goals (parents not causing the problem, but may be stressed and in need of extra supports)

Figure 2. Copyright 1998/2010 Dr Kay A. Toomey.

Q: How do you distinguish picky eaters from problem feeders?
A: Figure 3 offers some guidelines to distinguish picky eating from problematic feeding:

Picky Eaters:	*Problem Feeders:*
Have a decreased range or variety of foods they will eat; will eat at least 30 different foods	Have a restricted range or variety of foods they will eat; will eat less than 20 different foods
May stop eating foods due to "burnout" after a "food jag" but will usually begin eating them again after a 2-week break	May stop eating foods after a "food jag" that they do not begin eating again after taking a break, often resulting in a decreasing number of foods in the child's repertoire
Are able to tolerate new foods on their plate; can usually touch or taste a new food, even if reluctantly	Cry and "fall apart" when presented with new foods; demonstrate complete refusal
Eat at least one food from most food textures or nutrition groups (eg, purees, meltables,* proteins, fruits)	Refuse entire categories of food textures or nutrition groups (eg, hard mechanical foods,† meats, vegetables, soft cubes)
Frequently eat a different set of foods at a meal than the rest of the family (but typically eat with the family)	Almost always eat different foods at a meal than the rest of the family (and often do not eat with the family)
Add new foods to their repertoire in 20-25 steps on the SOS Steps to Eating Hierarchy	Add new foods in much more than 25 steps on the SOS Steps to Eating Hierarchy
Are sometimes reported by their parents as being a "picky eater" at child wellness checkups	Are persistently reported by parents as being a "picky eater" at multiple child wellness checkups

* Meltables are foods that melt in your mouth with saliva only (without applying pressure with the teeth), such as baby-cereal puffs and graham crackers.
† Hard mechanical foods are foods with a harder texture that need grinding or rotary chewing to break apart. Examples would be Cheerios, fruit leather, steak, and saltine crackers.

Figure 3. Signs of picky eating versus problem feeding. Problem feeding warrants further intervention from a feeding specialist. Copyright 2000/2010 Dr Kay A. Toomey.

Q: *What do you recommend for a family who is looking to have their child evaluated for feeding therapy? How do they find a trained therapist?*

A: There are a variety of ways to look for a feeding therapist. The best option is to go to the Popsicle Center's Web site *(www.popsiclecenter.org)* and take the screening questionnaire online. Then, bring the results to your primary-care physician and ask that person for a referral. The Popsicle Center Web site is also working on creating a list of various centers that provide evaluations and treatment for feeding, as well as a list of questions parents should ask when looking for a feeding therapist. If you want an SOS therapist, you can look on the STAR Center's Web site *(www.starcenter.us).*

In our first book, *Sensory Parenting: From Newborns to Toddlers*, we talked in depth about feeding and dietary concerns. We feel that this information is very important for all parents to review, so we've included that discussion for you in Appendix A at the end of this book for easy reference.

Another resource you might try as a visual learning tool is our DVD, "OT in the Home." This DVD walks you through a host of activities of daily living, such as eating, dressing, bathing, bedtime, and brushing teeth. Britt demonstrates several sensory-regulation strategies with children to facilitate a balance in doing these everyday tasks.

CHAPTER FIVE

Sensory Needs at School

A child's occupation at school is learning. This includes being able to attend to the teacher, read, write, complete assignments, engage with friends, navigate playground equipment, and function successfully in the school environment. Here are some things you can do as a parent to prepare your child for school each day:

- Lay your child's clothes out the night before.
- Make sure your child gets a good night's sleep.
- Eat a nutritious breakfast together.
- Incorporate sensory activities into your morning routine, such as jumping on a miniature trampoline, crawling through a tunnel, bear-

walking to the breakfast table, or giving your child a few squeezes on his shoulders to organize his proprioceptive system before he gets into the car or onto the bus.

- Have him drink thick liquids through a straw, as this will help calm his body and provide input to his mouth.
- Let him know the schedule for the day so he is not surprised if something in his routine is different.

Sensory Needs Inside the Classroom

If a child is having a difficult time performing a task, OTs are known for being able to get children to participate. We'd like to encourage teachers and administrators to consult their school's OT when a child in their classroom is not functioning well in the school environment. OTs can work with children in the classroom individually or with a group and guide them toward achieving independence.

In addition to working on a child's sensory needs, OTs work on social skills and functioning skills, such as task initiation, organization, sequencing, and problem-solving.

Movement

Children cannot sit all day and/or be contained in a classroom for 7 hours a day without doing some form of gross movement. Our bodies do not function well when immobilized. We need to have a wide range of movement and interaction with others and our environment to be able to function at our optimum level. When a child acts out or steps out of line in the hallway, too often this is perceived as disobeying the rules, when it really may be about a child's body needing to engage in gross movement to calm his sensory systems. As a parent, you have to advocate for your child and what he needs, even when he is at school.

Some teachers take away recess as a punishment when children have broken one of their rules. This can cause the child to act out even more, if he's not getting the exercise he needs to function. If a teacher must keep a child from recess, perhaps he or she could ask the child to perform tasks around the classroom, such as wiping tables, rearranging books, or dumping out trash cans—anything to get the child's body in motion. An alternative could be to have the child walk on the track outside or around the football field during recess.

For younger students, in kindergarten up to third grade, pretending to be animals is something fun and usually familiar to children. Bear-walking is a great weight-bearing activity for the hands and shoulders. This is also considered a vestibular activity, because it moves the fluid around the inner ear. An example of how to incorporate movement into a simple math lesson would be to ask each child to do a different animal walk up to the chalkboard to solve a math problem. Why? Because movement helps keep the children's attention on what you are trying to teach. As they move their bodies in space while you give them a concept to learn, it will oftentimes move into their memories more efficiently. Fourth and fifth graders, for example, will enjoy doing exercises like jumping jacks or reaching up to the sky and touching their toes. Teachers can gauge what motivates their particular class and work from there. There are various programs that incorporate movement into the classroom easily. Yoga is one way to have the children participate in movement in between or during a teaching lesson. Another program is called "Brain Gym." Many teachers use this program in the classroom with great results. Or, it can be as simple as having everyone stand up every hour to take a stretch break or do five jumping jacks and five push-ups against the wall. We know it is difficult for teachers to add anything else into their busy day, but the fact remains that if children are encouraged to include more movement, they will demonstrate increased attention and focus.

All children—not just those with special sensory needs—will benefit from "getting the wiggles out." A teacher can encourage the children to stand up and "shake it out." The kids can even do this while seated at their desks, if necessary. It is a fun activity for the children to do, and it incorporates a lot of calming, proprioceptive, and large (gross) movements that help children in many different ways, including organizing, increasing attention, and focusing their energy so they can sit and attend to a task.

Another thing that is great for children is jumping and moving at different speeds, because it increases body awareness and vestibular processing. Doing this while engaging in academics means the child is also working on following directions, auditory processing, and visual processing, to name a few benefits.

Individual Sensory Needs

While all children have different needs, it can actually be very easy to incorporate each child's needs into the classroom. If one child needs preferred seating to be able to see the chalkboard and reduce visual overload, then the teacher should be able to accommodate that. Another child may benefit from writing on a more vertical surface, such as a slant board, to make copying sentences or letters easier. Erasing a chalkboard or dry-erase board is also a good shoulder-extension activity for kids, and if they have to push down hard, it gives them some proprioceptive input to their shoulders, arms, and hands. If a child needs that extra input, the teacher can figure out ways to incorporate it throughout the day, so it benefits the child and doesn't disrupt the classroom.

Some children respond well to wearing a weighted vest, as it helps calm their bodies down. You can make one at home and fill it with little beanbags, or Fun and Function *(funandfunction.com)* has a wide variety of both weighted vests and compression vests. They also have lap pads with animal designs that the kids can put on their laps while they take a test, eat dinner, ride in the car, or use anytime they're feeling fidgety or anxious. The weight is calming, and the different textures of the pads provide your child with tactile input, as well. The most significant function of the weighted vests and lap pads is helping to center the child, so he can focus on the task at hand.

An important note is that a child should only wear a weighted vest for 20 minutes at a time. Then, he should take it off for 20 minutes. He can either put it back on, if it helps keep him regulated, or he can wait until the next time he needs it. The reason you don't want a child to wear a weighted vest all day is because his body will habituate to the weight and pressure, and after a while the vest will not be as effective. If a child uses a lap weight when doing seated work, he can use this as long as it's needed, but he should get up to take breaks from sitting and focusing at his desk.

If a child bites his nails in social situations or when he's nervous, one alternative is to have him chew gum. Some schools allow children to chew gum as long as they keep it in their mouths. If they abuse the privilege, they lose the opportunity to chew the gum. If your child has an IEP or a 504 plan and the team thinks that gum or another oral-motor chewy tool or source of input could be beneficial for your child, then you should talk to your OT about how much oral-sensory input your child needs. Then, you can work it into your IEP. Another alternative would be using Chewelry or a chew stick. Some teachers offer crunchy snacks to help children focus while doing hard tasks or when preparing for big transitions.

Fidget toys can help children focus as they work. A lot of times, squeezing a toy or fidgeting with it can help a child stay focused on the task at hand, especially if it is hard. Sometimes the toy can be too much of a distraction, and teachers need to be able to discern the difference so they can use the toys as needed. The fidget toys can also make a child feel more secure when he has something to do to occupy his hands. It can help work out his anxiousness and regulate his sensory systems.

Transitions

Some children have a hard time waiting in line. The teacher may notice that a particular child will always be in the front or perhaps the back of the line to avoid being touched by other children. The teacher could help this child by calling his name last for lineup or by just allowing the child to be the caboose as the children transition to the library or wherever the class is headed.

When transitions are difficult for children, such as moving from reading time to another activity, the teacher can give 5-minute warnings to alert the children that the transition is coming. Some teachers will dim the lights, in addition to giving a verbal cue. It can also be beneficial for a child to have a visual schedule, with pictures or a written schedule, posted in the classroom so he knows what comes next. This works well for all children, so they can prepare for the transition ahead of time.

Some kids gravitate toward leaning against a wall while waiting in line or waiting to return to the classroom after recess. This is a natural way to get deep-pressure and proprioceptive input, and by doing it they're calming and regulating their bodies. We know that some school personnel frown upon leaning against the walls in the hallways, but if they understood how this benefits the children, they might reconsider. Talk to your child's teacher if this has been an issue for your child. Another option is to have the children hop in place while they wait, alternating legs, to give them the proprioceptive input they require. Or, you could teach them how to give themselves hand squeezes. This can include squeezing each individual finger and especially providing pressure to the "web space" in between the index finger and thumb. This technique can be very calming for any time of the day. When we teach children calming strategies they can do themselves, they feel more empowered and have more control over their regulation.

Seating/Posture

If your child's chair cannot be lowered or raised, you can sometimes raise or lower the desk or table to make sure your child is sitting at the right height for tabletop activities. The child's hips and knees need to be at a 90-degree angle while sitting on a ball or in a chair. You can tape phone books together with duct tape and place them under your child's feet if necessary, so her feet don't dangle. A poor pelvic tilt disables a child's breathing, vision, and ability to pay attention. We recommend using chairs with arms whenever possible.

A wiggle seat (or "Move 'n' Sit") is recommended for kids to sit on while working on a tabletop activity. The slight movement of the seat actually increases a child's attention to task, since it engages the sensory systems. The movement initiated by the wiggle seat also encourages movement in all directions of the abdomen, which increases a child's core strength. This is necessary to maintain good balance. Depending on your child's preference, you can use either the bumpy side or the smooth side of the wiggle seat. This seat is typically a round shape, or it can be a wedge. If you use the wedged seat, make sure you put the larger part of the wedge toward the back of the chair and the smaller side right under your child's legs. You don't want to turn it the opposite way and increase the posterior pelvic tilt, where the child's knees and/or back of the legs are higher than her pelvis (hips).

Your child may put her chin in her hand while sitting at her desk, which is a natural human instinct that provides pressure and is calming for most people. Teachers will often tell a student to sit up and stop slouching when she rests her chin on her hand, but this is actually a good position for a child to receive information. If she's so tired that she falls asleep on her desk, well—that's another story.

You may also try placing a slant board on your child's desktop. Some children find the position of the slant board to be more comfortable, and it provides support for weak wrists and hands. Other children find that the "lift" of the slant board makes it easier to see, since the board brings the work surface closer to the face. This can provide a good transition for students who have difficulty alternating from a horizontal surface to a vertical surface when copying letters or sentences, such as when a child has to copy from a teacher's chalkboard onto her own paper.

At times, students may lie on their stomachs on the floor to do their lesson. Lying on the floor can provide deep proprioceptive input to the shoulders and upper extremities. Most classrooms have an area for circle time or presentations, which the kids can spread out on, but as students get older, classroom space is harder to come by.

It is okay for children to do homework in other positions, besides sitting in a chair. It's a personal preference, and if changing positions assists a child in getting his work done, then this is a meaningful and productive activity. Some kids can sit in chairs, some can sit on balls, and some can use wiggle seats or pencil grips. You can accommodate whatever your child needs in the classroom, but talk with your OT first about what he or she believes your child may need.

Gross-Motor Skills

Gross-motor skills are important for a child to develop before she can demonstrate good fine- and visual-motor skills. Typically, as children develop, they begin with gross-motor movements as infants and then move into more fine-motor skills. Many times, as OTs, we see children who have been able to accommodate to having decreased motor control and are able to demonstrate good fine-motor skills, but they still have poor gross-motor skills. We also see children who have poor motor skills all around. Our bodies need to have good postural control and co-contraction of our muscles for us to be able to do things like walk, run, ride a bike, catch a ball, sit in a chair, and write.

Figure 4. Working with a parachute can be a valuable gross-motor activity to do in the classroom.

There are many different gross-motor activities that can be done in the classroom. Working with a parachute is a great hand-eye coordination activity (Figure 4).

Using a parachute does involve a lot of movement, and some teachers are hesitant to engage students in large-movement activities in the classroom. But, it may be one of the best activities to do if the children seem restless either before or after a lesson. Of course it needs to be guided, and the students must understand that there are rules that apply to this kind of activity. However, the overall body movements serve a dual role of both calming and alerting the body systems as needed. Activities like this one can work wonders.

I'll give you an example: Think back to a long seminar, where you've been sitting for 3 hours. Wouldn't you have given anything for the speaker to stop and ask you to stand, stretch, and breathe deeply for 3 to 5 minutes? The alerting and calming benefits of taking a movement break are well worth the effort.

Balloons are a valuable tool to use with children. If a child has difficulty throwing, catching, or tracking objects visually, the balloon will float longer than a ball when it's tossed, and the child will have a slightly longer time to process and react. If you are concerned about the latex in the balloons, a volleyball can also be beneficial, because it floats slightly longer in the air than a heavier ball does.

Bubbles are also helpful. You can have your child try to pop the bubbles with one finger. It requires visual-motor and tracking skills to be able to follow where the bubble goes, reach a hand out, and pop it. You can have your child clap at the bubbles, which requires bilateral coordination. This can even be done during a transition time in the classroom. Yes, it might get the children's papers wet, but they can clear their desks before doing it or do the activity in the center of the classroom. Touchable bubbles are also good, because they last longer than regular bubbles and you can actually catch them with your fingers. This gives a child the chance to track the bubble visually, then motor plan how to reach out and get the bubble. These can make a little mess on the floor, but they are good for hard floors that can be wiped up. Better yet, use them outside. Touchable bubbles can be found online and in toy stores. We've even purchased them from Old Navy!

Fine-Motor Skills

There are many different types of pencil grips. It's best to consult with your school's OT to figure out the best writing tool for your child. Try to help your child grasp a pencil properly when she is young, so you do not have to fix an inappropriate grasp later. Sometimes, a poor pencil grasp is caused by weak hand strength. But, if your child has difficulty in this area, you also need to look at why your child has weak hand strength or poor writing skills:

- Does your child have good posture?
- Can she keep herself upright in her chair when she writes?
- Does she have good shoulder strength?

Instability usually starts more proximally—or closer to the body—than the hand and fingers. A trained OT can look at a child and assess whether she has weak hand strength or if it is really more of an underlying trunk or shoulder weakness.

Single-Finger Isolation

Single-finger isolation builds the intrinsic muscles of the hands and fingers. When a child has poor muscle strength or small hands, doing isolated finger exercises is a good strategy to increase the dexterity of the fingers. You can do this by using play dough, Gak, goop, or any media that children can use to work their hands, wrists, and arm muscles. Gak is made of glue, borax, and water, and the recipe can be found in chapter 9. A teacher could incorporate this into the classroom in many different ways, while practicing writing letters and numbers or drawing shapes with younger children. It is also a good warm-up or warm-down activity to do in the classroom.

Scissors

Scissor use is almost a discipline in and of itself. The first rule of thumb is to always have your child use the best scissors you can find. This is a tool that you want to spend money on. You can start by placing your hands over your child's hands and helping her get a sense for what using the scissors feels like. Use different textures of paper, cloth, and the like, depending on what you want your child to accomplish. Do you want to use scissors to increase hand strengthening? Do you want to use cutting as a visual-perceptual activity? Or, do you want your child just to have fun and snip at paper?

Try having your child cut therapy dough (or play dough). This is good for some children who are learning how to cut, as it gives their hands more body awareness about how to do it. The dough provides more resistance to their hands than paper does. Cutting strips of index cards or card stock is helpful, because it provides more stability while your child learns to cut. If your child has a great deal of difficulty using regular scissors, an adaptive pair of scissors might be in order. Talk with the OT at your school to see what is best.

Utensils

It is important to teach children how to grasp a variety of utensils, including pencils, crayons, tongs, forks, and spoons. One activity that is good for honing fine-motor skills is teaching children how to grasp tongs and control them. For instance, you can have your child pick up

Figure 5. Strawberry pickers or miniature tongs can help your child develop her grasp and fine-motor skills.

a small object with tongs and place the object in a jar. This also requires the use of visual-motor skills. Strawberry pickers (miniature tongs) are sometimes hard to find, but they are good to use to work on grasping and fine-motor control (Figure 5).

A Sensory-Friendly Classroom and Calming Area

Depending on how your child's teacher likes to run his or her classroom, having a sensory corner for children to use can be very beneficial. If the teacher sees that your child is having difficulty focusing and moves around a lot, perhaps she could allow your child to get up and retreat into a calming, quiet corner. Your child could engage in some deep-pressure and calming strategies, such as squishing beanbags, large pillows, or foam pads. Also, if your child does not follow the rules, the teacher can take that activity away. But, most children really enjoy having this calming retreat, so they will participate appropriately. And, as always, never leave any child unattended.

Calming activities are appropriate to do whenever the teacher believes it is necessary. You know your child better than anyone, and if you feel that a particular transition or subject is going to be hard, you can ask that your child be allowed to participate in a calming activity before starting the more difficult one.

Sometimes kids just need a break. One idea is to let your child sit on a giant beanbag to read a book or look at pictures. You could also provide some quiet music with headphones for her to listen to while she is drawing or just relaxing.

Q&A on Classroom Sensory Products with Aviva Weiss, MS, OTR/L

We asked pediatric OT Aviva Weiss to recommend sensory products for use in the classroom. Aviva is the president and cofounder of Fun and Function *(www.funandfunction.com)* and By Kids Only *(www.bykidsonly.com)*. Fun and Function offers versatile toys, games, and therapy products, and By Kids Only has comfortable kids' apparel that is soft and free of itchy tags.

Q: Which products do you recommend for a child who needs to learn to sit in a chair and attend at school?
A: For being able to sit and attend, I recommend:

- Having the child try an inflatable seat cushion.
- Sitting on a ball chair.
- Using a weighted lap pad, to help keep the child grounded.
- Making sure the child is seated at her desk properly, with her feet planted firmly on the ground and elbows at desk height.
- Having the child sit on the floor, maybe in a reading corner, as this can be "grounding" and improve the child's focus.

Q: *What about a child who needs help with his or her vision in the classroom?*
A: To help a child with vision, I would recommend:
- Brightly lined paper
- Raised-line paper
- Wikki Stix, an outstanding tool to create raised borders and/or kinesthetically teach letters and shapes
- Slant boards, which bring the paper closer to the eyes and can help children with poor vision
- MyBoard, a keyboard with large, bright, colorful keys
- A portable prism light center, a table lit from below so your child can trace and see better
- A Time Timer, to help a child understand how much time she has to complete a task
- A visual Time Tracker (electronic programmable timer)
- Desktop carrels (barriers), which help with visual processing and focus and narrow a child's visual space
- Multi-Matrix game

Q: *What sensory items do you think are most important for teachers to have in their classrooms?*
A: If I had to pick a few, they would be:

- Ball chairs, to allow movement while seated
- Seating cushions
- Weighted lap pads
- Beanbag chairs
- Fidget toys
- "Tune Up Your Mind" Music
- Noise-reduction headphones
- A Time Timer

- If space permits, a small, enclosed corner where a child can calm, regulate, and use sensory tools to self-calm

Q: What products can be used to calm your child before a test?
A: First, prepare your child in advance! Review the test information well, talk about the test expectations, and review the test environment—what the setting will be like. Talk to your child about her concerns. You can educate your child about any products that may be used to help her calm down before and during the test and discuss these products with her ahead of time.

Additionally, motor activities, especially those involving eye-hand coordination, will help your child be able to regulate and focus. Some examples of these activities are:

- Give a Flip
- Alpha Catch
- Space Explorer
- Resistance Tunnel
- Stretch Eze
- Visual charts for anxiety reduction
- Aromatherapy
- "Relax Daydream & Draw" Music
- Chewies for kids who need it—gum can be excellent!
- Compression tees and vests for children who are soothed by deep pressure

For the test itself, I'd recommend:

- Noise-reduction headphones
- Fidget toys
- Gum
- Chewies
- Weighted vests and compression vests

- A Time Timer
- A desktop carrel (barrier), to eliminate distractions

Q: *Can fidget toys be distracting in the classroom?*
A: It really depends on the setting, the teacher's style, the organization level, and the child's needs. If the fidget toys are distracting during learning time, it might be helpful to provide the child with a fidget toy during recess or break time, so her sensory needs are met on some level. I believe that there need to be enforceable "fidget toy rules," such as not throwing the toys and staying at your desk while using them.

Q: *What would you like parents and teachers to know about using sensory products in the classroom?*
A: There are some fantastic tools out there, but they should not just be given out haphazardly. It is recommended that an OT determine which sensory tools are needed for your child. Most sensory tools work well, if they are used intermittently, at specific times, and not just at random. There has to be a reason for the tools and a plan for using them. There also needs to be a behavioral orientation with any sensory tool provided, so the child understands its purpose, why it helps, and how to use it appropriately. I also recommend that teachers use their own tools, so they can be handed out as needed, and this way the teacher is in control.

School Drop-Off and Pickup

Have a plan for dropping your child off at school and picking her up afterward. If she needs time to play on the playground to work some energy out before school, drop her off early (and make sure there is a school representative on yard duty). If your child feels anxious before school, then leaving her early is likely not a good idea, as it may stress her out more. The playground in particular can be hectic and discombobulating. Instead, maybe it would be better to drop her off just as school is going to start or right before the bell rings. This way she can scoot directly into the classroom and start her day immediately, rather than stress out waiting in line or on the playground.

Chaos typically sets in after school lets out. When the bell rings, hundreds of kids pour out of the school at once. For underresponsive kids, this can be a joyful time of bumping into each other as the cattle drive moves toward the school buses. However, this time can be torture for overresponsive kiddos. They may become confused and not know where to go, if you haven't arranged a meeting spot. The end of the school day can be a nightmare for these kids. Perhaps you could pick a designated meeting area by a tree or in the front office. For kids that become paralyzed and overwhelmed, see if they can stay in their classroom with the teacher until you arrive (but be on time, as teachers are not babysitters!).

If you have an overresponsive child that rides the school bus, arrange to meet the bus driver. Join your child as she gets on the bus and becomes familiar with it. Find out if she will be wearing a seat belt, and talk with the driver about helping your child find a seat as she gets on the bus (most buses do not have assigned seating). Wait with your child at the bus stop, and be there waiting for her when she arrives home, if possible. Also, make sure she knows where to meet the bus after school. If there are multiple buses, it can be confusing for a child to get on the right one.

Lunchtime and Recess

Lunchtime is a big deal at school. If your child is socially awkward or has social anxiety, see if there is a "lunch buddy" program for your child to join, so she has a small group to eat lunch with. Some schools offer classes during lunch, or a reading group, or chess club. Often, if your child is doing an activity, then the stress of eating lunch with others is relieved, and she can eat peacefully. If there is not a "lunch buddy" program available, give your child something to do when she finishes her lunch. Perhaps you could send her to school with a game, some sports equipment, or an art project to occupy her. She may be able to use these activities to engage with another child. But, please don't send anything to school with her that will be detrimental if lost or stolen!

If your child is a sensory craver, make sure he can finish his lunch in plenty of time to get his energy out on the playground. Sensory cravers may be known to play rough, so set boundaries and make sure he follows the rules. These kids may need some direction, as well, so having a lunch-playground plan can be helpful. The more gross-motor activity your child gets during this break, the better he'll be able to focus during class!

Some children may be slow eaters or have difficulty with textures, flavors, or trying new foods. These youngsters may not want to eat at school at all, because it's so hard, and they just want to get outside to play. Or, they may not want to sit with their peers at lunch if they get teased. Make sure you know what is happening with your child at lunchtime, since this is a good time for kids to socialize and make friends. Sometimes, it can be beneficial for your child to eat in a quieter environment and then join his peers at recess afterward.

Bathrooms

Going to the restroom at school can be an ordeal. Everyone's body makes sounds and smells that can be embarrassing, and kids with sensory issues may not be able to tolerate a public restroom. Some kids will hold it in all day, so they can eliminate in the comfort of their own home. Others will wait until class is in session and ask to go to the restroom when it's empty, knowing they'll have more privacy. If your child has anxiety about using the restroom at school, talk with his teacher about choosing the optimal time for him to go. Holding it in all day can be painful and disruptive to your child, as it may prevent him from being able to complete tasks. And then, there are those dreaded accidents. If your child is prone to having accidents at school, always have some extra clothes for him in his backpack, with his teacher, or in the front office.

Also, make sure your child can dress and undress himself for these bathroom trips. If your son can't unbutton his jeans or unzip his jacket, he's not going to be able to have a successful bathroom experience.

Anxiety, Bullying, and Playground Politics

There are different types of anxiety that a child may experience in the classroom. Everyone may become excited or nervous when a test looms, or a child's palms may sweat over a sudden pop quiz. This is natural. It isn't until it becomes debilitating that it represents a problem.

Another type of anxiety is social anxiety. A child may feel nervous and afraid around other children and situations. He may be too scared to talk to the other children or to raise his hand in class.

Playgrounds are battle zones. There are rules and a pecking order that isn't taught—it's just inherently learned by the students. The drama that goes along with growing up is often saved for recess, and it can be stressful for any child.

If your child is having any of these anxieties at school, see if your school psychologist can help. At one school, we found a "Think It Through" class held during lunchtime, which helped students understand the rules of the playground. The psychologist who taught the class used puppets to act out common school issues, like cutting in line, stealing jump ropes and equipment, waiting for swings, chasing boys, and using insults and inappropriate behavior. Many schools are starting "lunch buddy" programs, where the teacher assigns a few students to eat together. Teachers know which kids have similar interests, and they can help the students work together. Some children complain that other kids cheat at soccer or kickball games, but they don't usually tell anyone, because they think the recess monitors won't do anything about it. Make sure you talk with your child about any issues that may be causing him stress at school.

Jackie's Experience with Anxiety at School

My son's extreme anxiety is often hidden. He appears to be a "normal" child, but then his anxiety can strike at unsuspecting times. In second grade, my son's teacher told me that he was "fine" and showed no signs of being anxious in class. Then, she decided to switch the children's seat assignments without telling them first. When my son had to switch seats, it was as if his world fell apart. He yelled, ran out of the classroom, and threw himself down on the ground, unable to cope with the change. My son's anxiety finally came out, and the teacher realized it was always there, deep down, ready to pop up and surprise her.

What worked well for my son and his teacher through the rest of the year was giving him warnings when there was going to be a big transition. He, in turn, learned to ask her about the schedule so he knew what to expect. I received e-mails from the school, letting me know about an upcoming fire drill or an assembly, so I could prepare my son before school. This type of communication made it a successful school year.

Something Special

Last, but certainly not least, to help my son deal with his school-related anxiety, each year I let him pick out something special. It usually ends up being some new pens or scented markers. While these items are unnecessary for school, I've found them to be vital for his confidence and ability to self-regulate. It's amazing how happy a hamburger-shaped eraser can make a child. Spend an extra dollar, and place the special item in the front of your child's backpack for times when your child is having a hard time at school.

One thing my son's psychologist suggested that worked well for us was to put some "rocks of love" in his backpack. I let my son pick out some colorful little gemstones that were "magical" to him, and we put them in a small pouch. I told him that every night I would kiss the stones and put my love on them, to surround him with a "loving force field" throughout the day. Having these "rocks of love" with him at school really helped him get through the day. Throughout the school year he would sometimes ask me, "Did you kiss my rocks last night?" Be open to anything that may make your child feel more secure in the classroom. If you try the rocks, make sure they're small, as you don't want to weigh your child down.

Kids and Technology

In this day and age, almost all children in elementary school take a computer class. It is important for your child to know how to type and use the computer. There are many typing games that your child can play to become a master typist. SpongeBob taught my son to type very quickly and accurately. "Type to Learn Jr" and "Type to Learn 3" are also great typing programs. Some computer games can be educational and help with cognitive skills, as well. It is still important for kids to know how to write and spell and look words up in a dictionary, but computer knowledge is required in almost every job out there today.

Some children have difficulty coming up with words and ideas when they write, and there are programs for the computer that can help. One example is "Co-Writer," which is a program that helps predict the word or phrase you are trying to type. It also helps with spelling and grammar. "Dragon Naturally Speaking" is a program that will type for you when you talk. This can be beneficial for anyone who has a limited ability to type with their hands, or even for those who are not as efficient at typing. The program trains itself to your voice so it can pick up what you're saying more accurately.

There are tons of computer programs that can help kids with math, reading, science, history, and more. Some of these programs can help motivate kids to learn if they do not quite "get" a concept in the classroom setting. There are also many useful "apps" that you can get for Mac computers and iPads, which can help children with academic learning.

Many schools have computers in their classrooms, or the teachers use "smart boards," where the students each use a remote control to respond during the lesson, allowing the teacher to track their scores. Other schools use iPads in the classroom. There are predictions that soon, children will download their books onto a personal electronic device rather than having to lug heavy textbooks to and from school. The times are certainly changing, and it's important to try and keep up so your child does not fall behind. Are you feeling the pressure? Maybe you can take your child to the local library and let him play educational games on the computer there, if you don't have one at home.

Sensory Needs Included in IEPs and 504 Plans

An IEP is intended to help children with deficits that affect their academics, social skills, motor skills, or sensory skills. Each state has different requirements to determine which children qualify for an IEP. If you feel that your child is not succeeding in the classroom, you can ask the school for an evaluation. Some children need to acquire an official diagnosis to be able to qualify for services; other times, they may qualify because they cannot keep up with the reading or math skills required in their grade level. If your child has deficits, some options include qualifying for assistance in the classroom, going to a resource teacher for help in a specific academic area, and receiving physical therapy, OT, speech-language therapy, or adaptive PE (a physical-education class for children with special needs).

A 504 plan is for children who may not qualify for an IEP because they are doing very well academically, but they need some accommodations in the classroom for motor, language, behavioral, or sensory needs. Ask your teacher, principal, or special-education teacher if your child needs additional assistance at school to help him succeed.

Developing social skills is an important part of school life, and this should be included in your child's IEP or 504 plan. If your child cannot learn to connect and work with other children, then he's not going to have a successful school experience. Also, paying attention to your child's level of sensory comfort will help him learn, keep up with the class curriculum, and excel. Don't be afraid to ask for what your child needs. Also, do your homework to find out how to word requests for what your child needs, so your school will accept the verbiage. Sometimes it can be best to ask for more than what your child requires, so you can eventually settle on what you really want for him. There is definitely strategy involved in maneuvering through your child's school career. I have found that most schools will work with parents who are reasonable. Be sure to point out the sensory needs that can be addressed in a way that will not cost them any money!

That said, you need to have realistic expectations for your teacher and your child's schooling. Teachers only have so many resources to go around. A stressed-out teacher is only going to add to your child's anxiety level, so don't overburden teachers with sensory strategies that are impossible to implement. Prioritize your list, so the teacher knows what is crucial for your child to be able to get through the day. Then, you can add what you'd like to tack on, if he or she is able.

If your child has an IEP, make sure the accommodations your child needs start right away. Accommodations can include taking sensory breaks, using fidget toys in the classroom, sitting on a Move 'n' Sit, wearing headphones if your child is auditory sensitive, or anything else your child may need. Sometimes, it takes therapists a while to get rolling with their large caseloads before they begin to see your child for direct therapy (where the therapist pulls your child out of the classroom to work with him) or consultation therapy (where the therapist treats your child in the classroom and consults with the teachers on how to help provide the right tools and strategies for your child). But, your child's teacher can at least start some of the sensory strategies needed. Hopefully, you have set this up in advance.

Educate yourself about your child's IEP. You need to know exactly what your child's goals are and which services he is receiving every week, month, and/or year. You have to advocate for your child, because he typically cannot do it himself. Make sure you talk about his specific sensory needs with every teacher and assistant that interacts with him at school. Here are some examples of how accommodations appear in an IEP:

- Child A will be taken to the resource room for test taking, away from other students, with the educator reading the directions out loud.
- Child B will be able to chew gum in the afternoons during math lessons.
- Child C may remove her shoes during lessons and wear flip-flops.
- Child D will have an OT in the classroom with him for 30 minutes each week to help him with writing and cutting.
- Child E will work with a speech-language pathologist 60 minutes per week to work on the articulation of sounds.
- Child F will be allowed to take sensory breaks as needed during difficult tasks at his table.

These are not specific goals—just ideas to demonstrate how an IEP could help your child if he qualifies. If you work with an IEP team at your school, the team members will write specific goals that are directly related to your child's needs.

Aides

To have an aide, or to not to have an aide—this is the question. The argument against an aide, besides being a financial stress on the school, is that a child grows too dependent on having the aide and may become isolated from the other children. Also, an aide might be good for a child that needs extra help in the beginning of his elementary school career, but the catch is that it has to be a good aide and not a babysitter. A good aide will encourage your child to participate with the other students. He or she may even facilitate contact with the other children in a fun way that gets them involved. A good aide is able to mask the fact that he or she is only there for your child and will help the teacher and perhaps the other students with tasks, as well, if the teacher feels that this is okay. In the end, you need to weigh the pros and cons and make the choice that is best for your child.

Advocating for Your Child (When to Bring in Backup)

There may come a time when you have done all you can to advocate for your child, and you feel that you need to bring in a professional. There are nonprofit organizations that have advocates to help you, or you may need to hire an attorney that specializes in IEPs and 504 plans. Don't do this out of anger or to show your school who is boss. Also, don't do it if it's not really necessary. But, as a parent, it is your right to get the services that your child is entitled to by law. Find a balance, and maybe talk to someone else who has used an attorney if you feel that you really need one. Once you start paying for an attorney's services, the costs can add up quickly for both you and the school district. Maybe it would be best to consult with an attorney first, to ensure that you even have a case.

For an overview of addressing your child's sensory issues when it comes to school, you can check out our DVD "OT in the School." We take you through a typical day at school and explain how any child with sensory needs can achieve success with transitions, seating and posture, fine- and gross-motor skills, using scissors, writing, and more.

CHAPTER SIX

Sensory Needs in the World

After-School Groups, Lessons, and Sports

Children in elementary school need activities, hobbies, lessons, and engaging interactions to be able to learn about themselves and the world. See what your child gravitates toward and try to strike a balance between activities, school, and home life. As you know, some kids will pick one interest, such as ice-skating, and dedicate themselves to it for a lifetime. Other kids like to dabble in art, music, and sports, maybe taking a few classes and then moving on to something new. You can do whatever feels right for your family.

On a sensory level, activities that promote a balanced sensory system include horseback riding, soccer, baseball, karate, swimming, dance class, social-skills class, and yoga. Pick activities that stimulate your child and require him to strengthen and use all of his sensory systems. Just think of how many systems are engaged when your child plays baseball: Vision is required to track the ball, bilateral coordination and motor planning skills are needed to run the bases, and hand-eye coordination enables him to hit the ball with the bat. Auditory processing allows him to listen to his coaches and tune out the hecklers. His uniform has a distinct tactile feel, and as he runs across the outfield to catch a fly ball, the proprioceptive input from running tells him where his body is in space. Baseball is also a valuable opportunity for your child to work on his social skills and sportsmanship!

Another example is swimming. Swimming helps develop many of your child's sensory systems, including the vestibular sense (moving through the water) and proprioception (getting deep-pressure input as he pushes his arms and legs through the water). He also gets tactile input from the feel of the water against his skin and olfactory input from the smell of the chlorine. In the water, he can work on motor-development skills, bilateral coordination, and balance. Just the feeling of floating in the water can be a pleasurable experience, or perhaps even a little scary.

Activities like these require your child's body to do a lot of work. Embrace them, and by doing so, you'll help your child's sensory systems develop successfully.

Autopilot Parenting

As a parent, you need to think carefully about how much independence you encourage in your child, versus automatically doing tasks for him. For example, are you doing your child's volcano report for him? How many choices are you making for him—perhaps too many? Are you packing his lunch, when he is capable of doing it himself? And, most importantly, are you cramming his afternoon schedule with activity after activity? Stop and think for a moment about how your child is supposed to learn to make choices for himself, if he doesn't have to or isn't allowed to.

During elementary school, kids learn to become more autonomous. While there's no need to go overboard with it, if you let your child make at least some choices at this age, it's a skill he will be able to take with him into junior high, high school, and beyond. Is your child hungry at school? Why not let him help pack his lunch? Does he want to quit Boy Scouts and join the swim team? Why not let him choose? Did he not finish his book report on Thomas Edison? Then maybe his teacher should deal with it, instead of having you finish the report for him. Bottom line: Kids have to learn how to make their own choices.

Now, it is possible for the pendulum to swing the other way. Some parents expect their kids to be miniature adults at this age—especially if they have older siblings. Elementary-school kids still need your guidance and will come to you for help with making choices. That, or they'll come to you for a hug when they've made a bad choice. Either way, this age is way too young to cut the cords of attachment.

Resist Rescuing

Parents of kiddos with sensory issues and other special needs have a tendency to rescue our children from most situations. Was it Nietzsche who first said, "What doesn't kill you makes you stronger," before Kanye West and Kelly Clarkson sang about it? While we use this extreme example in jest, hopefully you get the point. Our kids grow by learning how to deal with situations themselves. This was a tough one for me, as I always wanted to pave the road for my sensitive child. It wasn't until I started pulling back and letting him figure out how to deal with things himself that I started to see huge progress in his maturity. If your child is being bullied, then by all means, come to his rescue. But, if it's just a matter of standard schoolyard politics over who cut in line, then it's time for your child to start facing some of these obstacles on his own.

Too many parents want to do everything for their child, especially if he or she struggles with certain things. It's completely understandable. We truly believe that you have to find a balance that is best for your family. Just remember that the reason we have children is to raise them to be independent. If we continue to baby them too much, they will never learn. On the other hand, as we mentioned in chapter 3, some children are so emotionally delayed that going back to the basics and supporting their emotional needs can be very important. Sometimes, it takes an experienced specialist to help you figure out if there is a true emotional delay with your child and how you need to address it.

Anxiety

Some anxiety is natural. We all worry from time to time, and being fearful is the way we keep ourselves out of danger. But what if anxiety is a source of debilitation in your child's life? Some kids are obsessed with future events, and they try to control the environment around them. This anxiety can be paralyzing, especially during periods of transition or change.[11] Kids who are riddled with anxiety may become avoidant and choose not to participate in society. My child, for example, was an expert "deflector." He could remove himself from any situation like Houdini. So, what do you do if your child has anxiety attacks or phobias, and how does this affect his sensory systems?

Does your child live in a constant state of anxiety, even at home? My child couldn't be in a room by himself. He checked the doors and windows repeatedly, in an obsessive-compulsive fashion, to make sure they were locked. He also couldn't use the restroom alone. It was hard on us as a family, but it was especially hard on him. Thankfully, therapy with a sensory-integration approach helped decrease his anxiety levels as his sensory systems became rewired over time.

An important message that I convey to parents, which they don't like to hear, is, Your tone sets the mood for everyone in the house. Is Dad stressed from work? Is Mom panicking about having to fix dinner? Or maybe Mom is worried about paying bills, or Dad is upset that he got laid off at work. Our kids learn to regulate themselves from us. As a baby, your child's sensory systems are regulated when he lies peacefully on your chest. Throughout his childhood, you set the tone, and he mimics your actions. You have to calm down for your child to be able to calm down.

If you don't believe us, then maybe Daniel Siegel, MD, and Tina Payne Bryson, PhD, authors of *The Whole-Brain Child*, will be more convincing. According to this doctor duo, each of us has what is called "emotional contagion," meaning, "The internal states of others—from joy and play to sadness and fear—directly affect our own state of mind."[12] The authors state that we not only mirror those actions, but we have "sponge neurons" that react on the basis of what we see, hear, smell, taste, and touch. In other words, we soak up the behaviors, intentions, and emotions of others like a sponge.[12]

Sensory Systems and Anxiety

If your child's sensory-processing systems are not functioning, then his anxiety level may increase. For example, if your son can hear but is not able to process sounds and what they mean, then noises might startle him. If a toy fire truck at Target scares your daughter, she may become fearful of all Target stores.

Some children with sensory-processing issues are fearful of other children in general, but mostly when other kids are coming toward them. Kids are more unpredictable than adults, so sudden moves, loud noises, and unnecessary touching can be involved.

How Sensory-Processing Issues Contribute to Anxiety

Problem: Vestibular and Gravitational Insecurity

Is your child unable to walk in a straight line? Is he fearful of heights and playground equipment? Maybe he can't gauge curbs and stumbles into the street. This can be stressful, because he may get anxious about having to participate in physical-education class or bumping into other students' desks when he hands out papers in the classroom.

Did your child flail as a baby when you put him down in his crib? Is your child fearful of playground equipment? This may be caused by an issue with gravitational insecurity, where your child fears being unbalanced and having his feet off the ground. It can also be caused by an inability to process proprioceptive signals correctly.

Solution: Vestibular and Gravitational Insecurity

Encourage your child to swing on the playground to help get the fluids in his inner ears moving. Also, spinning may engage his sensory systems, but you want to make sure that your child spins a few times in one direction and then spins in the opposite direction, as well (such as in a swiveling chair or on a playground swing). This will help balance out his vestibular system without overwhelming it. You can also encourage your child to climb up just the lower steps of the jungle gym before he attempts climbing to the very top, so he slowly gets used to the sensations of climbing higher and higher.

You also want to slowly encourage your child to tolerate certain movements, heights, and positions, while supporting his sensory systems. Gently encourage him to climb on an uneven surface or swing with his feet off the ground. Pair these activities with heavy-work activities, such as carrying heavy items and doing push-ups. Incorporating "sensory-rich" activities like these can help a child with some sensory sensitivities. If his body does not seem to understand how to correctly interpret the sensory information that comes into his body, however, we suggest that you seek out an OT that is highly trained in occupational therapy with a sensory-integration approach.

~

Problem: Tactile Defensiveness
If your child is fearful of touching certain things with his hands, like paint or glue, then it will be upsetting when the teacher breaks out a new jar of pickles and wants the students to each pull one out.

Solution: Tactile Defensiveness
One solution would be if you provided a box of plastic gloves for your child, so he can cover his hands in times of need (with supervision). Another would be placing plastic Ziploc bags on his hands before playing with media like glue, paint, or Gak (again with supervision). Other ways to help a child become more comfortable with feeling various textures would be to slowly introduce him to things like bins of dry rice and beans, shaving cream, bins full of birdseed with favorite toys hidden inside, and brushing of the arms, hands, legs, and feet with various types of brushes. We suggest gathering up assorted items to create a "tactile box." Examples of items to include in the box would be soft brushes, loofah sponges, paintbrushes, squishy toys, Koosh balls, vibrating animals, carpet squares, and a variety of cloth samples from the fabric store. Then, allow your child to play with the items in his "tactile box" and brush these different textures on his skin to help him learn to tolerate the more nonpreferred textures.

~

Problem: Oral-Motor Concerns
Does your child drool a lot or have poor oral-motor skills? Does he have trouble figuring out how to bite and chew his food? Does he try to eat everything he can get his hands on—even nonfood items? He may have poor muscle tone or poor motor-planning abilities in and around his mouth.

Solution: Oral-Motor Concerns
Introduce your child to an assortment of chewy and crunchy foods. Obtain a Chewy Tube or other designated chewy for him to bite on, so he doesn't try to chew holes in his shirt. Chewelry bracelets and chewy necklaces are available at Fun and Function. As your child gets older, you don't want him to stick out from his peers as much. If he continues to drool, have difficulty holding liquids in his mouth, or demonstrate poor oral-motor abilities at an older age, seek out a feeding therapist for help. We'll talk more about feeding issues in chapter 9.

Problem: Proprioceptive Difficulties
Does your child have difficulty navigating around the classroom or house without bumping into objects? Is she unable to close her eyes and touch her nose with her fingers? If so, she may have difficulty discerning where her body is in space.

Solution: Proprioceptive Difficulties
Holding your child is important for proprioceptive development, and it helps her feel encased, protected, and comforted. Holding her also provides her with feedback about where her body parts are. Draping a weighted blanket or vest over her may give her the proprioceptive feedback she needs, as well.

For proprioceptive challenges, it is important to provide your child with opportunities to participate in heavy-work activities (see chapter 9 for examples).

Problem: Developmental and Learning Delays
Children with social and/or learning problems can have increased levels of anxiety, and the turmoil school brings often spills over into home life. Being behind the rest of the class creates not only added pressure, but stress, as well.

Solution: Developmental and Learning Delays
Make sure your child knows that while you want her to do her best, your expectations are realistic. Hopefully her teacher will be kind and accommodating, as well, to help decrease her anxiety levels.

Searching for the Root of Anxiety

If your child has chronic anxiety, talk to your OT and a psychologist about it. Dig deep. If medications are for you, then meet with a psychiatrist. As a team, these specialists should be able to address your child's sensory and emotional needs, thereby decreasing the anxiety. You have to make sure that you're addressing the underlying sensory concerns, in addition to providing anxiety medications, because just feeding your child medications will not fix the root cause.

When children exhibit anxiety, depression, or low self-esteem, a doctor may want to prescribe medications, but we believe it would be a better idea to seek out a specialist, such as a trained OT, to really get to the bottom of what is driving that anxiety, depression, or low self-esteem. A lot of the time, there are sensory issues that need to be addressed in addition to or instead of taking medications.

The Worst Thing You Can Do

Don't tell your child with anxiety to "Stop worrying." If it were that easy, she would. It's the equivalent of telling someone to just stop smoking or asking an overeater to lose weight. It's not necessarily easy to change our patterns—but we can do it. Just telling a child to stop does not help. Instead, teach your child coping skills. These are skills that your child will use throughout her life to help with any anxiety or panic disorders that may arise.

> **Mom Tip:**
> It's been said that rock stars eat bananas before a concert to help conquer performance anxiety. Eating two bananas around 30 minutes before showtime is supposed to decrease symptoms such as heart palpitations, shaking, and loss of concentration.[13] We suggest giving your little rock star a banana on days when she has an event that may increase her anxiety. Or, you could try making a banana smoothie.

Coping Skills

Breathing

Kids will hold their breath or hyperventilate if they're having anxiety. Have your child take a deep breath and count as she exhales. Count slowly, and encourage her to count, as well. Try giving her a straw to suck air through. This forces her to concentrate and slow down her breathing. Make it a fun straw or even a crazy straw, and keep it on hand if needed.

Another breathing activity is snorkeling. When you breathe through a snorkel, you can't help but be aware of your breath, and a child can work on controlling her breathing in and out. You can try this in the swimming pool, a lake, or even the bath. Having your child blow a pinwheel or a whistle also allows her to see and hear how she is breathing.

Talking It Through

Having your child talk to a psychologist about her fears can be very helpful, but you as a parent can also ask your child questions about how she's feeling and what her concerns are. You can talk about past events that may have upset her or future events she could be worrying about.

Daniel J. Siegel, MD, and Tina Payne Bryson explain that having a child tell a story about her anxiety can help the child make sense of what is happening. First, the child can name her fears, and then she can learn to tame them. These two specialists suggest that your child will be more inclined to talk to you if you're in the car, if you build something together, or if you do an activity together like play cards.[14]

Guided Imagery

Dr Charlotte Reznick's book, *The Power of Your Imagination*, is a wonderful resource for helping your child learn how to use her mind to calm herself, get a grasp on her fears, and move forward in a positive way. Dr Reznick also has CDs that your child can listen to that will guide her through breathing and calming exercises she can learn to do on her own. For more information, see *www.imageryforkids.com*.

Cognitive Behavioral Therapy

If you have a child with anxiety, you may have heard about cognitive behavioral therapy. Dr Tony Attwood explains that "Cognitive restructuring corrects distorted conceptualizations and dysfunctional beliefs."[15] In his workbook, *Exploring Feelings: Cognitive Behaviour Therapy to Manage Anxiety*, kids and parents can learn about their thoughts and emotions and how to restructure or replace the negative with the positive. He provides tools on how to fix "broken thoughts" to help manage anxiety. Dr Attwood has also written another book devoted to anger (*Exploring Feelings: Cognitive Behaviour Therapy to Manage Anger*). Maybe cognitive behavioral therapy could help you and your child. Check it out.

> **Mom Tip:**
> YouTube has been a lifesaver for me, because my child gets anxious
> about new things. These days, if we're headed to a baseball game, first
> we watch people at a game on YouTube. If we're going to try a new
> ride at Disneyland, guess what? The ride can be found somewhere
> on YouTube, so we can see what it looks like first. If we're going to
> take a field trip or go to the dentist, we watch YouTube together so
> we can talk about the experience and what to expect. (Note: Always
> supervise the content your child watches on the Internet!)

Arrive Early or Even Days in Advance

If your child feels anxiety about going to new places, try to arrive early and
let him settle in. Let's say you're going to attend a new church. Maybe you
can arrive early and allow him to walk around. This way he can familiarize
himself with the seating, the stained-glass windows, and the atmosphere.

This can also be a helpful tactic for your child at school, whether
she's attending a new school or starting a new school year. Visit the
school while no one is there and let her play on the playground. Look
for the bathrooms, find the water fountains, and point out the principal's office. You can go on a teacher's organization day and meet your
child's teacher—but make sure to schedule the visit, so the teacher
knows you're coming!

Online Anxiety Resources

Here are some additional resources you can use if your child experiences anxiety:

Anxiety Disorders Association of America, *ADAA.org*
Some of the features on the ADAA Web site include finding help from a

therapist in your area, understanding anxiety, living with anxiety, and taking action.

Worry Wise Kids, *worrywisekids.org*
This Web site talks about different types of anxiety and lays out the steps to take if your child needs help or treatments. It is a wealth of useful information.

Traveling

Planes

Most kids will find flying to be an adventure. The hard part is navigating through a crowded airport and then getting everyone through security (especially if a child has anxiety issues). If your child is anxious, has autism, or is just curious, then showing him videos of the security process before you leave home can make your trip a success. Here is a TSA (U.S. Transportation Security Administration) link where you can watch videos about air travel in general: *www.tsa.gov/travelers/airtravel/children/index.shtm*. This site also covers traveling with baby formula and breast milk, and, most importantly, traveling with children who have disabilities. Some children will want to watch the videos over and over again. Let them, as it will give you time to pack!

Does your child have food allergies? If so, you should plan on packing your own food for the flight (again, following TSA's guidelines). Don't pack a 16-ounce protein shake and expect to be able to take it on the plane. Don't bring a backpack full of sugary treats, either—you'll have a hyped up kid with nowhere to go. Stick with high-protein snacks and dried fruits, cereals, and easy items that aren't messy to eat.

Peanut allergies are still a hot topic with airline passengers. Even if you're on a peanut-free flight, there still might be peanut dust in the air, and some of the prepared food may have traces of peanuts in it. It's best if people with severe allergies talk with each airline about their allergy when they book their flight and again upon boarding for their safety.

Be sure to discuss take-offs and landings with your child, as the plane can be loud and scary. Bring headphones if your child has sensitive ears. The captain will speak over the loudspeaker, which can be a jolt if your child is just getting settled in. Neighboring passengers could also be loud, which might bother your sensitive one. Some planes can smell, and many are stuffy, regardless of the air being recycled throughout the trip. When landing, your child's ears may pop. Bring sugar-free gum or have your child drink water or eat a snack during this time to help alleviate any discomfort. If you have a child who needs a lot of stimulation and movement, we'll give you ideas about how to keep him occupied later in this chapter.

Trains

Just like with planes, even though trains may serve food during the trip, you'll still need snacks! Try and stick to your child's sleep schedule, and bring comforting items like blankies or stuffed animals. Even though most train trips include lots of sightseeing, your child will need entertainment to keep him busy. Also, the fast movement of the train could make your child nauseous.

If you're thinking of traveling by train, check out the Web site *wejustgotback.com* for tons of train traveling tips: *www.wejustgotback.com/default.aspx?mod=traintravel_kids*. Again, you might want to let your child watch examples of train rides on YouTube beforehand, so he becomes more comfortable with what he will be experiencing.

Motion Sickness

The skin, eyes, and ears constantly send sensory information to your brain. When your brain does not process the information correctly, nausea and sickness ensue. If your child is prone to having motion sickness, encourage him to face forward and look outside. Playing travel games and reading can worsen the symptoms. Talk with your doctor before attempting to use any medicines or homeopathic remedies for motion sickness.

Activities during Travel Time

On a road trip, there are always the classic "I Spy" games and "license plate bingo" to pass the time. Here's a link that lists 27 road-trip games you can play: *www.airlinecreditcards.com/travelhacker/27-free-games-to-keep-your-kids-entertained-on-a-road-trip.*

One of the great benefits of modern technology is that items like a Nintendo DS, a PlayStation, and a Game Boy will all get you through a few hours of travel. You will also need nontechnical items, like art projects, a new coloring book, and activities that will keep your child's mind and hands engaged, such as doing a lacing puzzle or even tying the laces on his shoes. If you have time, purchase some new toys before you go and hide them in your backpack. These toys don't have to break the bank—you can always get some knickknacks at the dollar store.

Movement

Your child is going to need to move around during a trip, which can be a challenge in cramped spaces like planes, trains, and cars. Plan on making at least a few potty trips, and use these times to work in some movement activities. If there's room, let your child get his wiggles out on the way down the aisle of the plane—he can jump, squat down and get back up, and stretch his arms. One thing that worked really well for us when my son was young was bringing a "play pouch" (Figure 6). You can make it yourself out of a Lycra fabric (that stretchy bathing-suit material is as strong as rubber). If you put your child's legs in it, the resistance will give him a great workout and provide the move-ment he needs while strengthening his legs. Just make sure he doesn't kick the seat in front of him.

Figure 6. You can make a "play pouch" out of a strong Lycra fabric and allow your child to push against it with his legs when traveling. The resistance will help him exercise his leg muscles in his seat and "get his wiggles out."

If you're on a road trip, plan on making plenty of stops to get out of the car and move. Look at your route ahead of time, and find the gems along the way—like the world's largest ball of yarn or a giant dinosaur. Even stopping to look at a field of flowers or taking a quick walk by a lake can be the most memorable part of the road trip. Here's a great link by RoadTrip America to help you find the stops that would interest your family most: *www.roadtripamerica.com*.

If your child gets motion sickness in the car, don't place him in the very back seat of the minivan. Be ready to open the window for a bit if he needs some fresh air to ease the queasiness.

Keep Yourself Regulated

Make sure you remember to pack your own favorite snacks and personal comfort items. There's nothing worse than a cranky parent on the trip to set the tone for everyone else. This is supposed to be a fun, memorable trip. Take pictures. Videotape. Your kids will grow up fast, so embrace the time you have to travel with your kids while they're young. There will undoubtedly be hiccups on your trip, and some things may go wrong. You may get a flat tire, but the kids will enjoy watching AAA come out and jack up the car. You may get lost. Turn it into a fun adventure. Just be sure to have enough gas in your tank! Your kids will argue, someone may have an accident, and at times everyone will be hungry and tired. If you get stressed, take a time-out for yourself. Have your partner watch the kids while you take a quick stroll. If you're the lone parent, take deep breaths and have quiet music time. Tell the kids that no one can talk while Mommy's music is playing. Figure out what works for you.

Disneyland and Other Theme Parks

Theme parks are amazing destinations for the entire family. Since we have frequented Disneyland, we'll use "traveling to a Disney park" as our theme-park example. Everything about a place where wishes and dreams come true is wonderful in our book, but Disney takes it a step beyond. Every time we go, part of the fun is watching other people's joy, and, more specifically, the joy of people with special needs. In a world where life can be cruel, uncomfortable, and unfair, at Disneyland, the playing field is evened out and perhaps even tips toward those with disabilities. It truly is a magical place.

Here are a few tips to consider if you're taking a sensory-sensitive child or a loved one with special needs to a theme park.

Disability Passes

Upon entering Disneyland, your first stop should be City Hall on Main Street. If your child (toddlers through teens and—yes—young adults too) has a physical or mental disability, Disney will give you a special pass. Call the park ahead of time to see if you need to bring any documentation from your doctor.

This pass allows you to enter rides through the special-needs entrance, which is sometimes the ride's exit and sometimes the fast-pace entrance. After a short while, you will get used to finding the correct entrance.

We don't always get the pass even though we can, but on the days when we do, the cast members treat you politely and you're never made to feel like a lower-class citizen because of the special privilege. Sometimes there will still be a wait, at rides like "Pirates of the Caribbean" or "Indiana Jones," but those rides are so popular that even the special-needs entrances get backed up.

What I really appreciate about the passes is that even folks with limited accessibility and those that have a difficult time and are uncomfortable on a daily basis can maneuver through the park and enjoy it as much as possible, in a shorter amount of time. Just think of how hard it can be for someone with difficulty walking to get around that massive park. Or how tiring it can be for a loved one to push a heavy wheelchair through the tightly packed crowds of people, all lost in their own agendas. Phew—it can be a lot of work!

Headphones

If you're bringing sensitive ears to the park, you must bring earplugs or headphones to buffer the sounds. There is always enchanting and delightful music blaring from speakers from every direction. While it works to keep you smiling and humming along, feeding your energy and somehow making you want to shop, it can be daunting to those with hearing sensitivities. I, myself, have found it to be mind numbing at times, since I can't tune anything out.

Crowds are loud. People are going to talk above the music and other people. Kids are going to scream, cry, throw tantrums, laugh, squeal, and make every other sound humans are capable of emitting. Parents scold their kids, talk on their cell phones, and sigh in exasperation. It can be a lot for anyone's sensory systems to take, but with earphones, you can tune them out and maybe collect your thoughts.

Fireworks, Shows, and Parades

There are theatrical musicals at the park, such as "Aladdin," which are glorious and intense. The actor's voices bellow through the auditorium, and the music is deafening, so those earplugs will definitely be needed for your sensitive ears. Remember to sit close to the aisle, in case you need to make a quick exit. Also, you can ask to sit in the middle of the auditorium to stay away from those powerful speakers in the back of the room and on the sides. The parades are a delight to watch, but, again, they can be loud. My son used to cover his ears every time a parade went by. He wanted to see Mickey Mouse skate past, but he didn't like all the noise. And then you have those magical, surround-sound fireworks. These are truly the most spectacular show in the sky, and I highly recommend jostling through the packed crowds in front of the castle to experience this truly phenomenal display. There is nothing like it—but, that said, those fireworks explode into the sky with a bang and pow, with a musical accompaniment that builds into a crescendo and a mesmerizing finale. Be prepared and wear headphones.

Sunglasses

Not only is Disneyland in southern California, where the sun shines most days of the year, but the park is also extremely visually stimulating. Every single place you look, there will be some kind of eye candy, and sometimes it can be too much for a child with special needs. For example, if something is spinning and very brightly colored, and your child is going around in circles on the "Dumbo" ride, then sunglasses may help tone it down a bit. Or, maybe the sunglasses will enable your child to be able to close his eyes at times and collect himself if he needs to.

Clothes

Unless you plan on purchasing Mickey Mouse sweat pants and a Tinker-bell t-shirt, bring a comfortable, dry set of clothes for your loved one. No one wants to sit in a wheelchair the rest of the day after getting soaked on Splash Mountain or racing through the fountain in Toon Town. Also, accidents happen, whether it is a potty accident or perhaps spilling lemonade down your shirt. Having an extra set of clothes often comes in really handy.

Shoes are so important at Disneyland. There is a lot of walking for you and your special-needs child to do. "Comfortable" and "functional" is what I recommend, and throw fashion to the wind. No one cares if you're wearing sneakers with a sundress. Be smart about your feet. If you're not wearing comfy shoes, the pain you'll have from walking around all day will reveal itself in your back, legs, and spine. If you're going to wear flip-flops, make sure they have a thick cushion. No high heels, ladies!

Not only can a hat keep out the sun, but it can also help keep your child regulated. That sensory pressure around his head can keep him grounded. Remember that Mickey Mouse ears do not protect your child from the sun! Also, if your child or loved one does get a sunburn, he may get dehydrated and grow more uncomfortable throughout the day. I for one have to be very cautious about my son's extremely sensitive internal systems.

Snacks

The parks are becoming more and more friendly to gluten-free, dairy-free, and sugar-free lifestyles. This is great news for everyone on a special diet, owing to sensitivities, allergies, or medical needs. I'm happy to report that we found gluten-free pasta over at the Pizza Port in Tomorrow Land. There are also gluten-free Minnie Mouse cookies and treats available. Rice Krispies treats in the shape of a flower, anyone? Yum. There are several sugar-free options for diabetics, and the park is covered with healthy options, such as fruits and vegetables. While the healthier options are now readily available, they're also expensive. So, unless you want to pay four dollars for an apple, bring your lunch.

Tips for waiting in line, no matter where you are:
- Play trivia games (either with the cards from the game or without).
- Mime (ask your kids to act out a scenario without using words). Be ready for the sillies.
- Play finger puppets (if you don't have a puppet, draw a face on your finger with a nontoxic marker).
- Balance on one foot (and other physical challenges). See who can stand upright the longest.
- Have a staring contest (a good excuse to look your child in the eyes). When was the last time you gazed into that little face?

Mom Tip:
Going to museums can be tough on some kids. If you're at an art museum and you want to add some fun, have an art scavenger hunt. Make a list of things for the kids to find in advance—a man with a hat, a woman with an umbrella, a black and white object, and a boat. You can create a list that is appropriate for their age and grade level. Bring clipboards and pencils for everyone, and be sure to give a prize to whomever finds the most items on the list. Or, better yet, have a small prize or treat ready for everyone. It will bring a whole new level of entertainment to the art museum.

Going to the Doctor or Dentist

I know that many children do not have any issues with going to the doctor or dentist. However, if you do have a child that objects, it can be a nightmare just to get him into the building. Some children associate the doctor's office with things that hurt, getting shots, or being sick, so it's not such a fun trip. Write a social story about going to the doctor or dentist, so he knows what to expect. Here is an example.

> On Monday, I am going to the dentist. Dr Wilder is very nice. He always gives me a toy when I am done being a big boy. I can be brave at the dentist, even though it can be a little scary. I know when I get there, I will have to lie down in the chair, and the assistant will put a paper napkin around my neck. Then, the dentist will ask me to open my mouth really big, so he can count all my teeth! I have a lot of teeth. I have even lost a few of my teeth, so the dentist will count how many big-boy teeth and how many baby teeth I have.
>
> After that, the nice assistant lady will begin to brush my teeth with a special toothbrush that tickles my mouth a little. If I get scared or uncomfortable, I can ask her to stop by raising my hand. I can also take a break from the chair if I need to.

You can even include pictures of your child at the dentist or doctor, insert the name of the dental assistant or the nurse that will be helping him, and have your child participate in writing the story to increase his comfort level.

Talk about what to expect, and after your child is done with the visit, reward him with a treat. Make sure you have a good, trusting relationship with your doctor or dentist, so you feel comfortable and your child does not pick up on your own anxiety.

Going to the dentist can be uneasy for your child, because the dentist has to get up close and personal in his mouth. What a weird feeling! And what is that tickly thing touching my teeth? Most pediatric dentists are very much aware of children's uncertainties and how to work with them to alleviate their fears. Talk to your dentist about your child's specific sensitivities and see what accommodations he or she can make. Sometimes, children need a little laughing gas to help them relax so they don't go into a complete meltdown. Your child may need a star chart, where he earns a star every few minutes for staying calm and allowing the doctor or dentist to do what needs to be done. Then, your child could pick out a prize at the end—like a new toy or some ice cream.

Always watch your child for signs that he is uncomfortable. In these situations, try to help him feel as safe as possible. For more tips on taking your child to the dentist or doctor, visit *www.spdfoundation.net*.

Pets

In our first book, we discussed having pets and the pros and cons of keeping different types of pets. We've added this section as an appendix (Appendix B) at the end of this book, to help you figure out which kind of pet would be best for your child. Pets are a big responsibility, so you want to do your homework and make sure you get a pet that is the right fit for your family.

SENSORY PARENTING: THE ELEMENTARY YEARS

CHAPTER SEVEN

Games

Play

Play is an integral part of childhood development. As humans, we use play to connect and reconnect after being apart. Play allows us to explore our environment, learn how to behave, and figure out how to do ordinary life tasks. We use play to help us cope, survive, and interact with the world. Play opens the door to our imaginations, our creativity, and our life's purpose.

OT Tip from Aviva Weiss:
In general, I recommend that you interact with your child continuously. This means making eye contact when your child talks and verbalizing direct responses to show that you are listening and available to meet your child's needs. Physical contact is also crucial. Children need to feel warm touches every day, whether it's hugs and kisses, a high-five, or a reassuring pat on the back. I also believe that you should spend at least 10 minutes each day engaging in a child-driven activity. This builds and enhances the relationship between you and your child and reinforces your child's awareness of his or her own abilities and interests.

Play can be many things. It can be creative, exploratory, and sometimes even competitive. Your child will likely play anywhere, anytime. Let him. Play with him in the car, at the store, and while waiting for your food at the restaurant. Why? Because play is a wonderful way to communicate with your child. Not all of life is a game, but when you're learning how to deal with life, it takes imagination to be able to create solutions. Play enhances our ability to make choices, communicate, and take turns. Play can be an extremely useful component in most life situations. Engaging your child in play encourages him to be a thinker. So much of life for a child centers around limitations and rules, but during play, he's encouraged to expand his mind and assert his individualism.

When it comes to playing with your child, your role as a parent play partner is very important. We addressed a parent's role in play in our first book, and have included some tips from those discussions in Appendix C.

🌹

Games

There are so many game options out there, it can be tough to pick which ones are going to be best for your child's development. If you're looking to work on a specific sensory need, we'll provide some suggestions as we go along. Some parents are wary about video games and especially 3D games, so we've gone to the experts and asked questions on your behalf.

What exactly is a game? Well, there are four defining traits of a game: the goal, the rules, the feedback system, and voluntary participation. The goal provides each of the players with a sense of purpose. The rules require the players to explore new avenues of possibility within a stated set of parameters. The feedback system of the game provides players with both promise and motivation, and voluntary participation means that everyone agrees to these rules and plays with free will.[16]

Golf is an example of a game adults play for their own intrinsic motivation. It has all four defining traits. Golf entails swinging a club at a little ball (the rules) in the hopes of sinking the ball in a predetermined hole in the fewest number of strokes (the goal). Counting the number of strokes, perfecting your swing, and having to maneuver out of sand traps (the feedback system) are part of the fun of the game. Last but not least, golfers are devoted to playing their game and often sign up to play weekend after weekend (voluntary participation).

The philosopher James P. Carse once wrote that there are two kinds of games: finite games, in which you play to win, and infinite games, which are undertaken with the goal of playing as long as possible.[16] Each type of game teaches a complex series of skills. Finite games have a beginning, middle, and end, while infinite games are more like life—they are continuous and involve players joining and leaving. Your child will most likely partake in many types of games, and it's your job to help put these challenges before him. Whether it's a store-bought game or one you make up as a family, playing games is an important part of life.

Game Night

Game night at home is an amazing way for families to bond. We still play board games in our home. We sit around the table while we play, and we talk about our day. Pick one night a week, or even once a month if you can't find the time, and enjoy some quality game time with your family. If everyone can't be there, that's okay too—but try. Perhaps you can take turns picking the game, or you can play two games in one night. It is a good idea to help your child feel successful while playing a game by occasionally allowing him to win to build his self-esteem. This is especially the case when he is younger, but you also need to help him learn how to lose, as well. It is important for your child to learn how to tolerate losing a game, so that when it happens with his peers, he will not "freak out" and melt down.

Video Games

Some parents believe that video games are a waste of time. Others think playing video games will hurt their child's brain or eyes. According to Jane McGonigal, author of *Reality Is Broken: Why Games Make Us Better and How They Can Change the World*, video games teach, inspire, and engage us in ways that reality does not.[16] Ninety-seven percent of our youth today plays computer and video games.[16] This is an extremely high percentage, which demonstrates that computers and games have become a mainstay in our society. While we know that most children and some adults play video games at some point in their lives, we highly encourage parents to also have their kids play outside and participate in gross-motor activities as much as possible. If children are going to play video games, we recommend more active games that require movement, such as Wii and Kinect. Also, we recommend that you limit your child's video game playing and require him to interact with his peers more often.

Q&A on Three-Dimensional (3D) Media Viewing
with Stephen Castor

Stephen Castor is the CEO of Rocket Science, a company that converts two-dimensional (2D) movies into 3D. He is an expert on all things 3D, and we talked with him about what exactly 3D is and how it works.

Q: *How would you explain 3D to parents who are curious as to what their children are viewing?*
A: In a 2D movie, a person's left and right eyes gather essentially the same information. Therefore, when the mind processes the information, the image appears flat, because there is no true perception of depth. If there is any 3D impression at all, it comes from visual depth cues within the image, such as perspective or a decrease in image sharpness due to depth of field and/or the presence of shadows.

However, we naturally perceive two distinct views—one with each eye—which our mind processes and combines into a single, "dimensional" image. This independent capture of two different angles of information (left eye and right eye) translates the visual cues that our mind uses to interpret depth. This way, we are able to perceive things that are closer to us (pulled forward) or farther away from us (pushed back). In turn, this allows us to visually understand the placement of items within our visual space.

With 3D technology, a distinct image is projected into each eye of the viewer, either through the use of glasses (stereoscopic) or without glasses (autostereoscopic). The viewer's brain processes each image in the same way it naturally processes the images it receives from the real world. The effect produces a true sense of depth from the media being viewed—a stereoscopic (3D) effect.

This gives the illusion of an object being projected out beyond the screen and coming toward you, or of an object being pushed down deep within the image, as if you were looking in at it through a window.

Q: Why do people get 3D headaches?
A: The headaches are caused by eye strain. When the 3D effects are overdriven, they are pulled too far "out of" the screen (toward and into the audience) or pushed too far "into" the screen. This causes eye strain, headaches, and/or eye pain because it creates severe eye convergence issues, leading to a bad strain on the eyes. The word *convergence* in 3D media means the crossing of your two lines of sight (the left eye and the right eye). Too much over- or undercon-vergence can cause eye strain. Remember, our eyes and brain work together as a sophisticated, real-time tracking unit. The eyes follow the movement, and the brain processes the incoming data. When a convergence issue occurs for long enough, it causes headaches.

Q: How do 3D televisions work?
A: To be able to view a 3D (stereoscopic) image, a person needs to see two independent images (one with the left eye and one with the right). Three-dimensional televisions work by displaying two separate images (one for the right eye and one for the left) either simultaneously and/or by flipping back and forth between the eyes very quickly. Most 3D televisions require 3D glasses as the delivery device. A delivery device is the method used to make sure that the independent images are displayed in the proper eye—one for the left eye and one for the right.

Q: The Nintendo 3DS is 3D, but my child does not wear the 3D glass-es. How is this possible?
A: The Nintendo 3Ds works in a similar way to a 3D TV. Instead of

using 3D glasses, however, there is a special lens and/or filter that is placed on the glass of the display. This lens or filter is what splits the imagery into an individual view for each eye (creating a stereo effect for the eyes).

Q: What do you want parents to know about 3D viewing?
A: As a parent, you should view some of what your child is watching and make sure the media is not being overdriven. If your child's eyes start to hurt while viewing 3D content, you should have your child stop watching to give his eyes a rest.

How Playing Games Can Benefit Your Child

When your child plays games, his sensory systems will likely be activated. He will learn about the all-important life lessons of winning and losing, to boot. Below are some games that stimulate a child's mind, as well as his sensory systems.

Board Games

- Sequence
- Chutes and Ladders
- Candy Land
- Monopoly
- Clue
- Parcheesi
- Checkers
- Life
- Sorry
- Family Feud
- Trouble
- Clue
- Totally Gross
- Boggle
- Jenga
- Headbands
- Cranium Jr

Problem-Solving Games
- Tetris (great for developing visual spatial awareness, speed, and accuracy)
- Qwirkle Board Game (a strategy game)
- ThinkFun Rush Hour
- "Hangman"
- Contraptions

- Snap Circuits
- Guess Who (a good way for kids to learn how to ask questions; to make it harder for older kids, you can have them write their questions down to practice writing)

Social-Skills Games
- Blunders (teaches children manners and how to treat others)
- Guess How I Feel (teaches children about emotions)
- "Charades"
- Apples to Apples
- The Story Book Game (teaches children how to tell stories from pictures and situations)
- Pictionary (playing on teams is a good way to interact with peers and family)
- Funny Face
- Story Cubes

Body Parts Games
- Operation
- Human Body J-I-N-G-O
- Scabs 'N Guts Board Game (also good for social skills)

Vision Games
- Puzzles
- Card games (any sort of card game, such as "Go Fish," Memory, matching games, and solitaire)
- Pictionary
- Connect Four
- Spot It!
- Nerf darts
- Bingo and animal bingo (picture matching)
- What's in Ned's Head (visual perceptual skills)

- Perfection (involves matching shapes with those on a board and working on fine-motor skills to put the shapes in before the time runs out)
- Cariboo (made by Cranium)
- Battleship (develops visual-tracking and fine-motor skills)

Auditory Games
- Bop It (great for sequencing, too)
- Simon
- Cranium's Hullabaloo (a small speaker gives instructions for kids to follow; this game is also good for the vestibular and proprioceptive senses)
- Scene It? (children must listen for clues in several of the tasks)
- Sing It (a video game for a Play Station, Wii, Xbox, or Kinect)

Fine-Motor Games
- Ants in the Pants
- Hungry Hungry Hippos
- Bed Bugs (increases hand strength and coordination)
- Tinker Toys
- Imaginets
- Dots-to-dot games
- Thread Art and Spiral Art

Tactile Games
- Hiding items in bins of dry rice and beans
- Goop, Gak, play dough, shaving cream, pretend snow, etc
- Texture dominoes
- Tactile discs (stimulate the tactile sense for both hands and feet)
- Ruff's House Teaching Tactile Set

Vestibular/Proprioceptive Games
- Twister (great for motor planning, balance, and body awareness)
- Outdoor lawn games, like bocce ball, BlongoBall, Frisbee golf, croquet, bowling, beanbag toss, and horseshoes
- Parachute games, played with a big parachute and several kids and/or adults
- Wobble Deck (also good for auditory skills)
- "Red Rover"
- "Duck Duck Goose"
- "Ring around the Rosie"
- "Chase"
- "Hide 'n seek"
- Four square
- Tetherball
- Hopscotch

Sequencing Games
- Puzzles
- Card games
- Bananagrams (develops vocabulary, spelling, and quick thinking)
- Rummikub (good for developing math skills)
- QBits

Body Awareness and Coordination Games
- Don't Break the Ice
- Wii games, such as Wii Sports, Wii Music, Wii Ski, Wii Ski/Snowboard, Wii Yoga, and Just Dance (gets your child up and moving, using both sides of his body)
- Kinect games, such as Body and Brain Connection, Kinect Sports, Dance Central, Twister Mania, Fruit Ninja, and Minute to Win It

GAMES

What parents need to remember is the importance of play. Play is not just a waste of an hour here and there—it is so much more than that, and it's crucial for a child's development and well-being. The next time your child plays, remind yourself of these points:

- Play develops problem-solving skills
- Play improves concentration, attention skills, and mathematical thinking
- Play helps establish neural pathways through repetition
- Play with peers encourages social development and emotional experiences

And the list goes on and on. So play and have fun. Both you and your child will benefit!

SENSORY PARENTING: THE ELEMENTARY YEARS

CHAPTER EIGHT

Sensory Seasons and Sensory Holidays

Winter

For those of us that don't live on a tropical island, winter means cold air and extreme weather, which can be extra hard on sensory-sensitive kiddos. Try to keep your child's skin from getting chapped by using nontoxic lotions on her body and lip balm on her lips. Remember that she may need sunscreen, even when it's freezing outside.

Severe cold weather can be painful for anyone—especially if you have SPD. If your child can only handle the cold for short periods of time, make sure she has a place to warm up if she gets too uncomfortable. Even a warm car will do.

Mom Tip:
If your child feels ill while she's out running errands with you during the winter, it may be caused by changing temperatures repeatedly. Going from the warm house, to the freezing cold outdoors, then into the heated car, then back outside again, and then into a warm department store can affect her sense of homeostasis. Just notice if you see your child getting more and more irritable as you pick out shoes.

Winter Clothes

New winter coats can be bulky and stifling, or, worse, too tight and constricting. It's best if you purchase a coat a size or two too big, and let your child grow into it instead of having it fit snugly right away. Don't forget that your child will be wearing layers underneath the coat, too. The texture of the coat is very important. Wool may keep you warm, but sometimes wool can be itchy. Think about how the fabric will feel if it gets wet as the snow melts. Remember that your child will be putting the coat on and taking it off again several times in one day to go to school, play outside at recess, come home after school, play outside before dinner, and so on. You get the idea. Make sure the coat is functional and that your child is able to maneuver the zippers and buttons by herself.

Take into account that in the winter, your child will likely need to wear layers. Again, soft, breathable fabrics are a must. When you're sizing gloves and mittens, make them snug without being tight. As tempting as it is to go big and have your child grow into these items, you don't want the mittens falling off her hands into the snow. You also have to remember to check the fabrics used and the seams, to make sure they're comfortable and that they don't get rough or soggy when wet. Scarves should be made with soft materials. If you can't find a good pair of earmuffs, you could even use your child's noise-reduction earphones to help keep her ears warm.

Mom Tip:
Can't get your sensory-sensitive child to wear a hat or scarf? Take her to the mall and let her pick out an animal-shaped hat or what-ever she thinks is "cool," and she'll be more likely to tolerate it. Or, start with trying to put a big silly hat on her during dress-up time, even if it's only for a few seconds. You can also try to get her to wear sunglasses on top of her head to help her get used to having something touching her head and ears.

Holidays

With the holiday season come many festivities—office parties, family gatherings, school plays, church celebrations, and more. All of these things can be a lot of fun, but they can also be hard on a child's sensory systems. Parties are often loud and hectic, or they can even be boring and stuffy. Either way, it's best to get your child's energy out before you arrive, so your child can regulate her body better. School plays can be a time to shine if your child is a ham, or they could also be very stressful for a shy kiddo. Having to wear a costume, memorize lines, and perform for an audience under bright lights can send a child into a sensory tizzy. Even family gatherings can be tough, with Aunt Marge's great big bear hugs, your cousin Eddie's five rambunctious kids who like to play with sticks in the house, the many smells coming from the kitchen, and the loud holiday music.

Try and gauge whether your child needs a break. This goes for sensory overresponsivity and underresponsivity, as well as sensory craving. Take your child to a quiet room, where she can have a snack or get a few squeezes and regulate herself. If a quiet room isn't an option, maybe walking around the neighborhood together or sitting in the car for a few minutes and listening to some music is a possibility. If she needs more time than that, then maybe consider putting on a movie or a TV show for her to watch, so she can relax for a bit.

New Year's

Oh what sweet anticipation, waiting for midnight to arrive (or earlier for the little ones). New Year's Eve is a festive holiday, with the tooting of noise-makers and cheering as the ball drops. Sometimes there are even fireworks and crowds, which can make for a raucous first few minutes of the year.

If your child doesn't do well in these types of situations, try and make it fun for her, so she can tolerate the celebrations and maybe even have a good time. Bring noise-reduction earphones, a weighted vest, and any other comfort items your child uses to regulate herself.

Mom Tip:
Each year, I come up with a theme for the kids that will be celebrating New Year's with us, to make it more fun for them. One year it was a glow theme, with glowing glasses, glowing maracas, and glowing ice cubes. This past year, we picked up beads and feather masks for a Mardi Gras theme. We even found a Mardi Gras game that encouraged the kids to socialize and exchange beaded necklaces. Everyone had a good time, adults and kids alike.

Get Outside

Sometimes rough weather prevents us from getting outside for some much-needed movement and sensory stimulation. But, here are a few motivators to help get your kids to weather the cold for a little while.

Frozen Bubbles

If it is cold enough outside, blowing bubbles is fun because the bubbles will freeze after you blow them and shatter like glass when popped. But don't worry, they won't hurt you or your child. What a delight to get that oral-motor proprioception by blowing bubbles this way! Surely, these magical frozen bubbles will entice your child to put on her coat and hat and get outside. Here is a good bubble recipe to try:

Homemade Bubbles
- ⅔ cup liquid dish soap
- 1 gallon water
- 3 tablespoons glycerine

Gently stir together and store in sealed container overnight.

Snow

If you're fortunate enough to live in a winter wonderland, there are many sensory uses for snow. Being that snow is so cold, you may not be able to get your youngster to play and work in it for very long, but here are some ideas to make the best of it.

Building a snowman is good fun for any child. Not only does packing the snow work her proprioceptive system, but moving around and focusing on the task helps her to self-regulate and calm her nervous system. Making snow angels, shoveling, sledding, and throwing snowballs are all fantastic activities to engage your child's sensory systems. By making snow angels, her entire body gets feedback from the pressure of moving the snow around with her limbs. Throwing snowballs at a target requires the use of her vestibular system and will help her work on her hand-eye coordination.

If your child is brave enough to try ice skating or hockey, these activities will help her work on her bilateral coordination, in addition to her other systems. Just think of how many systems have to communicate for a child to swing a hockey stick at a little puck while skating! Plus, you have to do this while other kids are coming toward you. It's a lot to coordinate! If these activities are overwhelming for your child, perhaps an evening at the roller rink would be more fun for her, where it's more organized and people aren't tackling each other.

> **Mom Tip:**
> You can have your child color the snow outside with spray bottles filled with water and food coloring. The squeezing of the spray bottles assists with the development of fine-motor skills and strengthens her hands, arms, and shoulders for handwriting.

Indoor Winter Activities

Sensory tables are an amazing way for kids to experiment with textures. Most often, they're filled with either sand or water or both, but you can fill them with almost anything, such as fake snow, shredded paper, marshmallows, ice (you can even freeze plastic animals in small containers or ice cube trays), packing peanuts, cotton balls, white sand, white rice, salt and glitter, real snow, or oatmeal. They're pretty easy to clean, as long as you don't mix too many things in at once! You can even make your sensory table smell good, with cinnamon sticks, powdered cocoa, a small pine tree branch, or some pine essential oil.

Indoor gardening is a fantastic way to bring the outdoors inside. We have found it easiest to plant a windowsill garden, with herbs such as basil, rosemary, lavender, oregano, and thyme. Choose durable plants so that even in freezing weather, some plants will be able to withstand the low temperatures.

Obstacle courses aren't just for outside! You can use furniture to make a course for your child to navigate that will help with his sequencing, behavioral organization, and gross-motor skills. Show him how to hop around the couch, crawl under the coffee table, push a ball through a Lycra tunnel, and then pick up three playing cards from the kitchen floor. You get the idea. Be creative and use what you have available. As long as your child is moving around in a safe environment, it's good for him!

Crafts are ideal activities for stimulating your child's sensory systems. Don't have time to organize a craft? Luckily for you, there are many crafts available for purchase. Science kits teach chemistry or how to make gum. Art kits enable a child to make bracelets or paint a tile. You can also make crafts with everyday items from around the house, like empty egg cartons, toilet paper rolls, water bottles, and shaving cream. All of these activities will stimulate not only your child's mind, but also his tactile system.

Here's a simple craft your child may enjoy—making a homemade snow globe! First, obtain a small, clear bottle or jar (a baby-food jar or a spice jar works nicely, and having a tight lid is mandatory). Fill the jar ⅓ full of corn syrup. Fill up the rest of the jar with water, and have your child mix the two as the corn syrup dissolves (yes it will be messy, so maybe stir it over the sink or make sure the table you're working on is covered first). When the corn syrup is all dissolved, top off the jar with water.

Sprinkle in the glitter. Use as much as you'd like. Then add beads or sequins! Secure the lid on the jar so it's good and tight, and allow your child to shake it up and watch the "snow" swirl around.

Baking is a sensory activity from beginning to end, and it works many sensory systems as once. When you make cookies, you put the ingredients in a bowl and stir them up, which makes use of your fine-motor skills, gross-motor skills, and proprioceptive system. If you make sugar cookies or gingerbread men, rolling out the cookie dough is hard work! Cookies can smell good, or burnt, depending on your oven, and there are many textures available to decorate them with. It can be good practice for your child to work with the icing, frosting, and tiny sprinkles and decorations.

Indoor camping can be a lot of family fun. You can set up the tent in your living room or bedroom and break out the sleeping bags. Turn off lights, and you can use flashlights or glow sticks to see. You can give each other squishes or deep-pressure massages, while telling ghost stories or princess stories.

Valentine's Day

This holiday can be sweet and fun—or it can be a sensory disaster. Here are a few tips to make it a great day for all sensory types. Remember that it's all about love—love for your significant other, parental love, friendship, and even love for yourself.

Why oh why do people make holidays about unhealthy food and candy? The surest way to not feel good and have your children bounce off the walls is to center the holiday around sugary treats. In our house, we try to make the day special with a homemade card or note and tell the people we love something special about them. That is worth more than a box of chocolates any day.

Also, these days there are plenty of healthier treats to choose from. While they're not exactly good for you, they won't make you feel sick, either. Gluten-free/casein-free cookbooks are full of delicious cakes, cookies, and pastries.

Since my son is still young, we get him a Valentine's Day present instead of sugary candy. This year he got a Pillow Pet. The soft red fur and heart-shaped nose delighted him. Last year, we got him a similar plush toy—another gift that kept on giving all year round.

This Valentine's Day, my son's teacher sent home a list of names so kids could bring in valentines for everyone in the class. On the note it said, "No peanut treats." I think that's great. With the amount of children who have serious food allergies these days, it's just safer. We just question why they need treats at all. Maybe cards with inedible goodies can suffice? With childhood obesity running rampant, not to mention allergies, asthma, and diabetes, maybe candy isn't the way to go. That said, there are plenty of candies that are gluten free and casein free, as well. Just read labels so you know what you're giving your child.

Affection

Let's talk for a moment about expressing feelings of love. For most kids, we can never oversell the importance of showing affection for your child and giving him hugs and kisses. Children love to show affection for each other by holding hands with their best friends or greeting each other with a tight squeeze. But what if your child is hypersensitive, and a hug is torture? Or a kiss feels like being licked by a St Bernard? And what about those people who squeeze so hard, you feel like you're being suffocated?

I remind my son to know and respect his boundaries. He'll tolerate a quick hug, although he'd prefer to go without. He avoids sensory seekers, who roughhouse and give hard high-fives. On holidays, when he knows we'll be getting together with other people and having to greet them, he prepares himself for plenty of physical contact.

In these situations, you could try and desensitize your child by putting him in a compression shirt to give him a nice, snug feeling, or perhaps you could apply some deep pressure to his shoulders and arms beforehand to help regulate him. If your child is a sensory seeker and you know he'll be attending a Valentine's Day party at school, maybe you could have him jump off the couch onto a crash pad before school or spend a few minutes on the trampoline before he heads out the door.

Also, what if you're married, or in a relationship, and you and your significant other have different sensory needs? It can create an intimacy challenge when the two of you aren't on the same sensory page. A great book to help you understand yourself, your partner, and how to come to a sensory compromise is *Living Sensationally*, by Winnie Dunn, PhD, OTR, FAOTA. Winnie identifies four major sensory types: seekers, bystanders, avoiders, and sensors. By taking a questionnaire in the book, you can figure out which category you fall into and then equip yourself with useful information on what will work best for you and your partner. It's a lot easier to understand your needs and those of others when you know that it's not personal, and it's not a choice. It's just a matter of sensory preference!

Spring

Here comes the rain. In addition to the spring flowers, the rain brings wet clothes, extra layers, rubber boots and jackets, hats, and umbrellas. Make sure your sensory-sensitive kiddo has a dry set of clothes to put on, including dry shoes and socks. Nobody likes to wear cold, wet clothes all day.

Late spring and early summer also herald the beginning of the stormy season. The howling wind, thunder, and heavy rainfall can be daunting for an auditory-sensitive child. Sometimes, the rain can create an offensive odor over a septic tank. Having moldy, damp places in the house can aggravate a sensitive child. Come up with a "sensory plan" for your child to be able to implement throughout the rainy months, in case the weather kicks up. Having a comforting place of refuge, with pillows, blankets, and music can make a big difference.

St Patrick's Day

On St Patrick's Day when my son was little, I used to put green food coloring in the toilet water and little puffs of green glitter around the house. When he woke up in the morning, he was delighted to see that the leprechauns had come in the night. If your youngster wants to join in the St Patrick's Day fun, here are some ideas you could try:

1. Go on a rainbow hunt, and have your child search for preselected items that are red, orange, yellow, green, blue, and purple.
2. Put on some music and dance like a leprechaun—surely it will involve some silly moves!
3. Mine for gold. If you live an area that has a gold mine that kids can visit to discover rocks and minerals, this is a good day to make the trip! If you don't have anything like this nearby, you can make your own gold mine. Fill a wooden box or bucket with mud. Toss in some pretty rocks about 1 inch in size that your child can "mine" for. If you don't have rocks or stones that would work well for this activity, you can go online and purchase rock kits, minerals, and fossils for your child to "dig up." You can mix the rock kit into your bucket of mud and then add some water on top. Your child can use a sifter or even his hands to find the special rocks. This can be a fun way to motivate your sensory-sensitive child to dig for treasure.
4. Make green eggs and ham. If your child is able to eat food coloring, try using a little to turn your child's boring breakfast into a storybook extravaganza. If your child is super sensory sensitive, this might put him off, but if you read Dr Suess's book before breakfast, it may encourage him to try something new.

5. Make your own air freshener! Gather some of your favorite essential oils and a 1-ounce spray bottle. Your child gets to choose how many drops of essential oil make the perfect blend. Then, he can come up with a name for his scent and decorate the bottle with a personalized tag. An example could be "Springtime Sass," made up of a combination of pink grapefruit and vanilla. Yum!

Summer

Summer break is the best. Along with summer break, however, comes the heat. Many kiddos can wilt in the scorching temperatures (although dry heat can feel more bearable than humid climates). It can be hard on anyone's system to go from extreme heat to freezing-cold air-conditioning. For a sensory-sensitive child, the cold salt water at the beach can be painful, and anyone who has ever had a sunburn knows how badly those can hurt!

Summer Sensory Tips

Here are some tips to make your summer plans go more smoothly:

- A more gentle way of getting sand off an itchy child is to sprinkle his skin with baby powder.
- Try brushing your child's skin before applying sunscreen to desensitize it first. Try to apply the sunscreen at home, before you leave the house. It's less of a battle, and the sunscreen will dry before you get to your destination.
- In addition to applying sunscreen, wearing sun-protective clothing and using umbrellas can help keep your little one safe from sunburns. Sitting in a tent on the beach is also a good idea to protect against too much sun exposure.

- Hydrate, hydrate, hydrate. If your kids are in the pool all day and not drinking fresh water, they can become dehydrated.
- Let the kids be fish! Swimming is such a wonderful proprioceptive activity for children and yields many benefits (as detailed in chapter 10).
- Take advantage of all of the fun water toys on the market. Slip 'n Slides are an amazing way to get sensory input. Try out a crazy sprinkler or just turn on your water hose!
- Creating chalk art on the driveway will keep the kids busy while you read your latest romance novel.

Mom Tip:
Play "Kerplink" or "Kerplunk" with your child. This can be played at the beach, at the lake, or even in your backyard. Fill a bucket with water, and have your child drop things into it—such as small rocks, shells, and seaweed (nothing massive that he could hurt himself with). He has to listen to which sound it makes—either a "kerplink" or a "kerplunk." For a complete list of great sensory ideas, visit the "Training Happy Hearts" blog *(traininghappyhearts. blogspot.com)* and look for the entry titled, "A Summer Sensory Diet Series: Kerplink-Kerplunk for Sensory Summer Fun."

Fall

Fall weather is unpredictable and can change throughout the day—from cool to warm and back to cool. For a sensory-sensitive child, layers are a necessity! The transition back to long sleeves, pants, socks, and shoes begins. If you have a child with sensory issues, the feeling of wearing long sleeves, pants, and socks may aggravate his tactile system and perhaps his other systems, as well. Toward the end of the summer months, you may want to gradually introduce him to shirts with three-quarters sleeves or put him in capri pants or jeans in the evening, when it's not so hot, so he doesn't go a full 3 to 4 months without wearing a pair of long pants. Also, even in the summertime, have him wear socks and tennis shoes—especially when he plays on the playground or runs around outside. You want to keep him accustomed to the feeling of wearing socks. Talk with your OT about ways to alleviate tactile defensiveness. One method is brushing the skin, where you use several different types of brushes to brush your child's arms, legs, hands, and feet. We do not recommend a certain protocol for brushing. You can use paintbrushes, vegetable brushes, a loofah scrub, and other soft brushes of many kinds.

Halloween

Once your child begins to get used to the weather changes and adjusts to his new clothes, it's time to begin thinking about Halloween. Putting on a costume for any length of time can be challenging for a child who doesn't like to wear extra things on his body—including hats, masks, face paint, and gloves. However, you can try and adjust his costume to help meet his sensory needs. Make sure he wears soft, seamless clothes underneath the costume. Limit the extra pieces that bother him, and hand-sew his costume when you can, because that way you (or he) can pick out the fabric. You can also allow him to try the costume on several times before the big night, so he gets used to the feel of it.

Hopefully he loves his costume and is excited about trick-or-treating, but maybe he's not looking forward to getting too close to anything (or anyone) really spooky. If this is the case, go trick-or-treating before it gets too dark, only go to a few houses, and pass up the ones that are all decked out. You could even talk with your neighbors beforehand and explain that your child has sensory sensitivities. You can request that they talk softly to him when he comes to the door and try to avoid scaring him.

One fantastic thing about Halloween is that it's a great excuse to do some sensory-processing exercises! Your child's sensory systems will be on high alert with all the excitement, and he will most likely be up for having some real fun. Here's a good tactile game we like to do, which helps develop stereognosis, or the ability to recognize and perceive objects on the basis of tactile cues. In this activity, you pretend you have purchased a witch's body parts to make a homemade stew!

You'll need:

- Brown paper lunch bags
- Grapes (frozen)
- Cold cooked cauliflower
- Dried apple slices
- A whole pickle
- Popcorn kernels (not popped) and dried garbanzo beans
- A tomato, blanched, peeled, and chilled
- Chopped carrots
- Cold, cooked spaghetti over cold, oiled cooked rice
- Parmesan cheese

Looks like a yummy recipe, right? Don't worry, no one will be eating the contents. They are intended for tactile and stereognosis purposes only.

Put each item in its own brown paper bag. Have each child feel around inside the bag before passing it along to the next child. You can have each child describe the items to make the activity more exciting. You will no doubt hear squeals of delight as their imaginations take over. Here is what each ingredient is supposed to be:

1. The cold cooked cauliflower is the witch's brains. The parmesan cheese is optional, to add some smell.

2. The two peeled, frozen grapes are her eyeballs.
3. The dried apple slices are her ears.
4. The pickle is her warty witch nose.
5. The popcorn kernels and dried garbanzo beans are her crooked, rotten teeth.
6. The cold, blanched, peeled tomato is her witch's heart.
7. The chopped carrots are witch fingers.
8. The cold cooked spaghetti is her veins.

After all the children have felt what is in each bag, you may reveal the contents that are really in the bag—or, you can keep it a mystery until next Halloween.

Thanksgiving

Thanksgiving is a time to be thankful for what you have in your life. This can admittedly be difficult when you have child with special needs. When I was growing up with my younger sister, who has a genetic syndrome and cognitive delays, I remember thinking I was grateful to have her as my sister. Then, as I grew into a teenager, it was harder to be thankful. I think this was because I was embarrassed of her, as any teenager can be.

When we have a child with special needs, we have to deal with therapies, medications, diets, special classrooms, schools, doctors, specialists, and more. This is why we, in particular, need to take a step back and take a look at what we are thankful for. Everyone has a different road to travel, and every road comes with its own set of twists and turns. But, I want to challenge you to write down the things you love about your child (or children). Write down his strengths and what makes him special.

I ask the parents I work with to do this exercise, and it's nice to hear them say wonderful things about their son or daughter. After that, we begin talking about their child's particular challenges and how occupational therapy can help him or her. I know that you probably talk a lot about your child's challenges and how you want to help him have a better life. But, remember that you are his family, and your most important job is to love him and care for him.

SENSORY PARENTING: THE ELEMENTARY YEARS

CHAPTER NINE

Sensory Activities

There are many sensory activities for you to do with your child. For example, a child that loves to spin and move constantly, jump and crash, and give hard high-fives is a child that seeks vestibular and proprioceptive input to his body. His treatment plan should address these needs and include tactile, auditory, and visual input, as well. If you only provide him with the sensation he seeks, he will habituate to this and it will not be as effective. An ice skater is a perfect example—she can spin and spin and not get dizzy because she has habituated to this vestibular input. You don't want your little one to do this.

An obstacle course is one of the best activities to do with a sensory craver. Put him on a swing (any type) and move him in various directions. You can have him sit on the swing, lie on his stomach, and stand up. Then, he can "frog jump" over to the miniature trampoline and jump and crash onto the large crash pad. Next, he can crawl through a tunnel back to the swing and start over again. This provides him with various types of sensory input while giving his body some of what he seeks.

An overresponsive child may get scared on an elevator, cover her ears when a car drives by, refuse to get on a swing at the park, or complain about her uncomfortable clothes. This child needs a specific sensory program that slowly provides various types of sensory input to help modulate her system and raise her threshold. This needs to be done with a trained OT.

An underresponsive child is hard to motivate—a couch potato. This child takes longer to register sensory input and needs a specific sensory program to help lower her threshold and make her feel things more quickly or more normally.

A combination of sensory-rich activities is required to help organize a child's sensory systems and modulation. This may change from day to day and from hour to hour. Every child is different, and you will always want to consult a qualified OT before developing a treatment plan for your child.

Sensory Activities (How to Help Your Child)

Here are some things that your OT might do with your child or instruct you to do. Please be sure to talk to your child's physician and/or therapist before doing any sensory exercises on your own. These are intended not to replace therapy but to give you an idea of what types of sensory activities may help.

Sight

Vision therapy is sometimes used by doctors in addition to or instead of corrective lenses. Vision therapy is used to improve vision problems, learning problems, recovery after a traumatic injury, autism, and even performance enhancement for athletes. Sometimes occupational therapy and vision therapy are combined. An OT will work with your child on sensory-integration activities, while the vision therapist will provide eye exercises. Daily treatment with both OT and vision therapy can yield dramatic improvements in just a few weeks' time.

An ophthalmologist can test the health and structure of your child's eyes and determine if your child can discern letters, shapes, and colors. If your child appears to have difficulty with visual-perceptual skills, eye tracking, eye coordination, or depth perception, then she needs to see a developmental optometrist. This is a doctor who looks at how the brain processes what the eye sees and determines if the eyes are working together. Sometimes, children can benefit from having special lenses or prisms in their glasses, or they can do vision exercises to train their eyes to work together. Occasionally, a child appears to have visual deficits, when really there is an underlying vestibular deficit. If this is the case, a trained OT needs to help the child work on her sensory systems either prior to or during the receipt of vision therapy. Please make sure you consult with your doctor or OT before doing any specific vision exercises.

Britt's Success Story

I worked with a young boy who was almost 2 years old and not yet walking. When you placed him on the floor, he cried and crawled to a corner, where he sat with his back to the wall so he could see everything in the room. If you placed him on a mat on the floor and he tried to crawl off of it, he screamed like he was going to fall 10 feet, even though the mat was only about 1½ inches off the ground. This child refused to swing and did not like to be moved. He wanted to be held tightly by his mother at all times. He was a triplet and was born prematurely. He did wear glasses prescribed by an ophthalmologist, but he still seemed to have extreme difficulty with processing what his eyes saw. I referred him to a developmental optometrist, and she confirmed that he was seeing the world at a slant, which was of course very scary for him. She put prisms on his glasses, and 2 weeks later he was walking! He also came for occupational therapy two times per week, and he began to trust his environment more. He started talking more and was able to discern that the 1½-inch-high mat was not a dangerous distance off the ground and that he wasn't going to fall. We still had to focus on his vestibular system and increase his tolerance for movement, but eventually he began to love to swing. Instead of screaming through therapy, he began to run to me and hug me when he came to the clinic. He also began to really look at the world around him. He looked up at other people, said hello, and tried to make friends. It is amazing what changes we can make for a child when we find the right solution to the problem. I would have never been able to do it without the help of the developmental optometrist. It was a true team effort!

Examples of Things to Do for Visual Deficits

Visual Tracking
- Play "flashlight tag." In a dark room, chase the light of a friend's flashlight as it shines on the ceiling and walls.
- Trace pictures. Place tracing paper over the pages of a coloring book or a picture book. Then, have the child trace the pictures underneath. Tracing favorite characters is motivating![17]

- Have your child use her eyes to follow an object left to right, up and down, and diagonally.

Visual Focusing
- Have your child string beads or make jewelry.
- Make a collage. Cut out pictures from old magazines and/or newspaper advertisements. Have her glue them to a paper or poster board.
- Work puzzles.[17]
- Use a Hart Chart to develop accurate eye movements.

Eye-Hand Coordination
- Throw and catch a ball.
- Play darts (Nerf has soft darts that won't hurt anyone or damage walls).
- Do archery.

Additional Vision Resources

Developmental optometrists can be located through the American Optometric Association at *www.AOA.org*. You can learn more about vision therapy at *www.visiontherapy.org* and convergence information at *www. convergenceinsufficiencey.org*. The following books may also be helpful: *Eyegames: Fast and Fun Visual Exercises* by Lois Hickman and Rebecca Hutchins and *Eye Power* by Ann M. Hoopes and Stanley A. Appelbaum.

Hearing (Auditory Processing)

If you're concerned about your child's hearing and believe it may be interfering with her ability to function, we recommend either Auditory Integration Therapy or the Integrated Listening Systems program. We talk about both more thoroughly in chapter 10. Additionally, your OT may suggest that your child wear noise-cancellation headphones if she has auditory sensitivities.

If your child is trying to focus on her homework and has a hard time ignoring outside sounds, providing white noise from a fan or noise-reduction machine may help. White noise is also soothing when your child needs to unwind and go to sleep.

Music therapy may be an option for your child. In a recent German study, researchers found that music therapy helped decrease tinnitus, or constant ringing in the ears.[18] Music therapists often work hand-in-hand with speech-language therapists on improving speech and providing nonverbal ways of communicating.[19] They also work on improving attention span and the ability to stay on task.[19]

Things to Do at Home for Auditory Processing

- Play the "Freeze" Game. Play some music, and have your child dance with you. Stop the music and say, "Freeze!" Time how long it takes your child to stop moving after you tell her to "freeze." This is how long it takes for your child's brain to receive the message, process it, and send the signals to her body to stop moving. Remember this time delay when you talk to your child. (In general, you want to give your child a direction once, wait to allow her to process it, and, if she does not respond, give her the verbal direction again. If she still does not respond, go and physically assist her, as she may not be processing the instruction you have given her. If you constantly repeat yourself, over and over, your child can become overwhelmed and get upset, because her auditory system cannot process that much information. Every time you repeat yourself, she has to process the information again.)

- Recognize that less is more. When you speak to your child, do you drown your message in a bunch of unnecessary talk? If you want your child to put on her shoes, do you say, "Jenny, please get your shoes on"? Or, do you go on and on: "Jenny, we're going to be late for your dentist appointment and then I have to go to the grocery store. If you had your shoes on already, we could be out the door and in the car. Your Aunt Vera is waiting for us at the post office." Keep to the message if you want your child to hear you. It may not be that she's not listening—she may just be tuning you out because you're giving her too much information.

- Even though your child is growing up, she may still need verbal cues before transitions. Give her warnings about how much time she has to complete a task to help facilitate the coming transition. If she's deep into her favorite video game, give her a 5-minute warning so she can save her game. If she knows that she has to stop playing and can wrap it up, you may have an easier time getting her to come sit down at dinner without both of you getting upset.

- Facilitate active listening. When you talk to your child, make sure she understands what you're talking about. Ask her to repeat the general idea of a story or idea, directions, or what you just asked her to do. You'll sometimes be amazed by how much she retained. Other times, you may feel peeved by just how little she was listening to you. If she's started ignoring your requests, maybe you need to switch up what you're talking about, or maybe you can add a little humor or unexpected silliness into your demands. This is guaranteed to get her attention and will sometimes help her listen better.

- Have quiet time during the day. Some children need a lot of help being quiet. They need to be able to be silent at school and listen to their teacher. We're sometimes so worried about getting our children to talk that we forget that being silent is also a skill they will need throughout life. This was a hard one for my son, so we started by being silent in the car. I'd say, "Okay, we're going to be silent until we get to the grocery store." It took months before my son could be quiet for an entire half-hour car trip, but surely his teachers appreciate that he's able to be still in class for a lesson.

Additional Auditory Resources

If your child is having auditory difficulties, you may want to consult with an audiologist, otologist, and/or an ear, nose, and throat physician. You can also visit the American Speech-Language-Hearing Association Web site at *www.asha.org* for more information, as well as the National Institute on Deafness and Other Communication Disorders Web site at *www.nidcd.nih.gov.*

Learn more about Auditory Integration Therapy at *www.aithelps. com/AIT_FAQ.html,* and perhaps look into listening programs that may help your child. Listening programs can be great, but be careful of burned copies! Every time a CD is burned, it loses quality during the convergence process. By using a burned copy of a therapy CD, your child could receive decreased sound quality and possibly glitches, static, and other discrepancies from the recommended audio program. Books you may find helpful are *When Listening Comes Alive*, by Paul Maudele, and *When the Brain Can't Hear: Unraveling the Mystery of Auditory Processing Disorder*, by Teri James Bellis.

Smell

Your child's olfactory neurons send signals to his brain through two pathways—the nostrils and the area from the roof of the throat to the nose. If these pathways are blocked, such as when he has a cold, then the ability to discern flavors is lost.

The Importance of Smell

At times, the first warning signal that something is wrong can occur via our sense of smell. Examples would be if we smell smoke from a fire, if food smells rotten, or if we detect the odor of dangerous fumes. Sometimes a loss of smell can occur as a result of a recent illness or injury, or it may even be a sign of a more serious medical problem. A loss of olfactory sensitivity may lead to depression, as we all know that smell can very much affect our pure enjoyment of life.

Things to Do at Home for Olfactory Processing

- Play "Name the scent." Use nontoxic products for this game. Blindfold your child and then hold a lemon, some coffee grounds, a jar of pickles, and other scented items up to your child's nose to see if he can guess what scent it is. You may also use essential oils on cotton balls, if your child is uncomfortable wearing the blindfold. It's okay to put some pungent smells into the mix, but be careful not to use any harmful chemicals. You might try rotten eggs, dirty gym socks, or vinegar if you want to include some unexpected smells. Introducing some unpleasant odors could help your child learn to tolerate them if he tends to gag or melt down whenever he encounters them.
- Play "Smell the roses." Take your child to the local grocery store or to a florist's shop. Have him smell the flowers. Talk about which ones are more fragrant and which scents he finds appealing. You can also do this on a walk around your neighborhood in the spring or at a local floral garden.
- Play "Smell by memory." Ask your child to pick a memory and then describe the smells he associates with it. For example, ask him to list three scents he remembers from going to a baseball game. Some examples might be the yummy hot dogs at a food stand, a foul smell from the restroom, and the smell of cut grass from the baseball field.

Additional Olfactory Resources

If your child is experiencing difficulty with his sense of smell, you might consult an otolaryngologist, an OT, a neurologist, a chiropractor, or even a nurse who is certified in clinical aromatherapy. The National Institute on Deafness and Other Communication Disorders is also a good resource at *www.nidcd.nih.gov*. You might also check out *Navigating Smell and Taste Disorders*, by Ronald Devere and Marjorie Calvert, and *Remembering Smell: A Memoir of Losing and Discovering the Primal Sense*, by Bonnie Blodgett.

Taste and Oral-Motor Function

We're extremely aware of oral-motor dysfunctions in our children, because they affect how a child eats and communicates.

Is your child a chewer? My son chewed holes in his shirt and came home with his shirtsleeves sopping wet. Or, maybe your child bites his nails or chews on his pens and pencils. Some children are teeth grinders, and they don't even realize it. The mouth is the organization center for neurological input for the nervous system and is a key player in regulating the body. Kids may chew when they're trying to regulate themselves better. Giving your child Chewelry, crunchy snacks like pretzels, or gum will keep his mouth busy so he doesn't chew on inappropriate objects.

An oral aversion is a reluctance to put something in your mouth. Babies can be reluctant to put things in their mouths because it makes them feel bad. It is not a willful response; rather, it is a learned reaction.

If your child has a slight defensiveness to new foods and/or textures, you can try the following at home:

- At each meal, encourage your child to try something new (this goes for young babies, who are eating baby food, as well as older children of any age).
- Allow your child to touch and feel the foods on his plate. It's okay to be messy!
- Encourage finger play with other types of media, such as finger paints, play dough, and other textures that are sticky or gooey (these activities should always be supervised and never forced).

Oral-Motor Interventions to Help with Overresponsivity

If your child is overresponsive to oral stimulation, is defensive about having anything in or around his mouth, has not been fed orally for a length of time owing to medical issues, or is orally sensitive for any other reason, here are some activities that you can do.

Use a warm washcloth to massage his gums gently. Allow him to chew and gnaw on the washcloth to get input on his gums and in his cheeks. Use vibration on the outside of his face and mouth by using a vibrating teether, a vibrating toothbrush, and even your own finger and hands to vibrate his cheeks and the area above and below his lips. Be careful not to overstimulate your child with vibration, as he may be resistive to this at first. Sometimes, as a therapist, I will even use a toy that provides vibration to a child's cheeks, neck, and shoulders, so I can touch inside and around his mouth.

OT Tip:
You can work on improving your child's readiness for a meal by encouraging him to eat crunchy and chewy foods that provide deep pressure to his mouth (proprioceptive input). This can help decrease the chewing of nonfood objects and putting inappropriate things in his mouth. You can also have your child blow bubbles, whistles, and pinwheels.

Additional Oral-Motor Resources

A speech-language pathologist or an OT that specializes in sensory feeding will be able to help your child with oral-motor concerns. You can visit *www.popsiclecenter.org* for more information. We also recommend the book *Just Take a Bite*, by Lori Ernsperger and Tania Stegen-Hanson.

Touch and the Tactile Sense

Therapy sand, or Moon Sand, is a fantastic medium for working on finger and hand strength. It can also be used in a bucket or a sensory table to work the upper extremities and abdomen. Children get quite creative with sand, and it can provide good tactile input. If your child does not like sand, start with long-grain rice or navy beans, which have a smoother texture but do not provide as much resistance. No matter which media you use, if your child is resistant to touching the media, have him drive a car through it or use sandbox tools to interact with it at first. You can try slowly introducing him to birdseed, cornstarch and water, bubbles, shaving cream or bath foam, and "flubber." (We will give you a recipe to make "flubber" or Gak later in this chapter.)

Working with beanbags can help improve bilateral hand coordination, attention to task, problem-solving, organization, and visual perception. You can use different types of beanbags, so your child is able to feel different sizes, textures, and weights.

Painting with paintbrushes can be a very useful fine-motor and visual-motor activity, as your child holds the brush with a functional grasp and learns to paint different strokes with the brush. Let your kiddo be creative when making art projects. If he will touch the paint, using his fingers gives him great tactile feedback. (When finger-painting, make sure you use safe, nontoxic paints.) Sometimes, children are unsure of touching sticky or gooey things, and finger-painting can be motivating and a fun way to help desensitize them so they'll try touching these types of textures. They can start with just their fingers and then move up to getting their whole hand in the paint.

Sensory fidget toys have many uses. They can motivate kids who are tactile defensive to experiment with different textures—like slimy, soft, and squishy. You can put baby powder on them to change their texture or place them in tubs of rice and beans so the child experiences multiple sensations at once. Some of the sensory fidget toys are good for hand strengthening.

When a child is defensive toward certain types of tactile input, it can affect his ability to function. Some children are sensitive to tags in their shirts, touching sticky or gooey things (like glue or finger paint), walking barefoot in grass, or feeling a light touch. Others may really crave touch and even want to touch everything they walk by, which can get a child into trouble at school.

You may have heard of the Wilbarger Brushing Protocol. I have used this technique a lot in the past. But, I have recently decided that it is best not to follow a specific protocol when it comes to brushing, because there is not enough research behind this specific protocol of brushing every 2 hours. However, I do still use brushing techniques with my clients. I suggest using a variety of brushes and teaching a child how to brush himself, so he can control how it feels on his skin. Loofah sponges can be good to rub on his skin in the shower, followed by a good rubdown with a towel afterward and a massage with lotion. All these techniques can help decrease tactile defensiveness.

When you are working with a child who is defensive to certain tactile input, the best way to approach that sensitivity is to not focus on the tactile system initially, but to target the proprioceptive system, instead. Give the child heavy-work activities, like doing wall push-ups, jumping, crashing, crawling through a ball pit, carrying heavy objects, rearranging furniture, and so on. As you focus on providing proprioceptive input, think about incorporating vestibular input, as well. Giving your child the opportunity to create an obstacle course with various types of equipment, either at home or on the playground, can help him experience various types of sensory input to organize his sensory systems.

Sometimes children can learn to start touching certain types of media they wouldn't touch before, but they still won't touch or eat certain foods. If this is the case with your child, you can have him play with foods like pudding, ketchup, and yogurt. He can dip foods like carrots into ranch dressing. If some of the dressing touches his fingers or hand, have a wet cloth ready to wipe him off if he gets upset about it. Our skin is our largest organ, and the information we receive from our skin tells us a lot about our environment. It can be easy to have a fight-or-flight response with certain tactile input.

Additional Tactile Resources

For further information about tactile sensitivity, visit the SPD Foundation Web site at *www.spdfoundation.net*. You can also check out the American Occupational Therapy Association site at *www.aota.org*. The books *Touching: The Human Significance of Skin*, by Ashley Monagu, and *The Out-of-Sync Child*, by Carol Kranowitz, may also lend some insights.

Vestibular System

Each of us stimulates our vestibular system naturally, when we sway to music or rock a baby. Indoor swings may be installed to provide linear movement for a child who needs help with vestibular sensory processing. One type of swing is a hammock swing, which the child can lie in by himself or with pillows and blankets. Swinging provides a fluid movement to the body systems and establishes a calming sense for most children. It is okay for the child to sit in the swing and do other activities at the same time, if he is comfortable in this "homemade cocoon." He can read a book and even do his homework in the swing by using a lapboard. Sometimes this movement and relaxing environment can even help a child focus on his homework.

A note about swings: You must follow all safety instructions when securing an indoor swing support bar and attaching the equipment. Never leave your child unattended when he's using the swing. Consider placing floor mats underneath the swing and clearing the surrounding area. Especially at first, you must "spot" your child and use appropriate safety techniques. Please read and follow all of the manufacturer's instructions.

Other vestibular activities to do at home:

- Jumping
- Playing "Stepping Stones"
- Walking
- Spinning (Be careful that your child doesn't spin constantly. Also, you want him to spin in both directions.)
- Walking a balance beam
- Climbing ladders
- Sliding down ramps
- Hanging upside-down (If he likes it.)

Make sure you try to pair vestibular activities with other activities, especially "heavy-work" proprioceptive activities. You don't want to increase your child's arousal level too much.

Proprioception

The proprioceptive system is stimulated via receptors in the joints and muscles, through movement and heavy work. When these receptors are activated, body awareness improves, and a person knows where his or her body is in space. Children who tend to crave proprioceptive input may overstuff their mouths with food, give hard high-fives, color with so much pressure the crayon breaks, and crash into things. Other children may hold a pencil so lightly that you can barely see the lines they draw, or they can't grip the pencil well enough to get it to stay in their hand. They may also have poor body awareness and bump into things or have a low tolerance for pain and cry at even the slightest bump.

When your child appears to be craving proprioceptive input, you want to provide him with some heavy-work activities, as well as some other types of input.

When we talk about heavy-work activities, I'm talking about:

1. Carrying heavy items (baskets filled with toys or books or bags of groceries—just not the bread or the eggs!).
2. Doing push-ups against a wall.
3. In the classroom, placing chairs on the desks at the end of the day or taking them down at the beginning of the day.
4. Erasing or washing the chalkboard or dry-erase board.
5. Wearing weighted vests, belts, and wrist weights. (When your child wears a weighted vest, have him wear it for only 20 minutes and then take it off. If needed, you can put it back on him again after a 20-minute break.)
6. Doing yard work, including mowing the lawn, raking grass and leaves, and pushing the wheelbarrow.
7. Doing housework, including vacuuming, mopping, and watering the flowers.
8. Taking chewy candy breaks—there are lots of chewy candies that take a while to chomp and won't get stuck on the furniture. (Please be cautious of giving your child too much sugar, though, and make sure he brushes his teeth afterward!)
9. Jumping on a trampoline and crashing onto a crash pad.
10. Wearing a weighted backpack when walking from class to class at school. You can also put a notebook, a book, or several books

(depending on the size) into his backpack each day for the ride or walk to school. Be careful not to put more than 10% to 15% of his body weight into the backpack, and make sure wearing the backpack doesn't cause him any lower-back pain. If this is a concern, you can try other things instead.

11. Sucking pudding or applesauce through a straw.

12. Tying a Theraband around the front legs of a chair, which he can kick with his legs.

13. Doing animal walks (like the "crab walk," the "bear walk," and the "army crawl").

14. Placing heavy quilts or a weighted blanket on your child at night. Make sure your child can pull it off himself, if needed!

15. Pushing the lunch cart or carrying the lunch bin to the cafeteria.

16. Swimming. Also, have child your dive into the pool to retrieve weighted sticks.

17. Sitting in a beanbag chair during silent reading time or lying on top of or underneath one during independent work tasks. This will allow your child to change positions and experience the benefits of consistent pressure input, especially if he is permitted to use one intermittently in the classroom.

18. Having your child pinch, roll, and pull Theraputty prior to doing seated work. You can also have him use hand exercisers or squeeze balloons filled with flour. He may like the sensation of firm pressure applied to his shoulders.

19. Playing the "Hot Dog Game," where your child lies across the end of a blanket and you roll him up in it. Or, you could squish him up in a crash pad.

20. Playing "Johnny Sandwich." Have your child lie on a crash pad, mattress, or blanket. Ask him what he likes to eat on his sandwich, and squish his arms, hands, legs, and feet while you pretend to put mayonnaise, mustard, turkey, cheese, peanut butter, or jelly

all over his body. Be sure to touch his head and face gently if you put "toppings" there. Then, ask him where else he needs toppings and have him tell you where his body craves more deep pressure. Make sure to press evenly and not too hard, as you don't want to hurt him.

21. Playing "Push Fives," where you and your child put your hands together in a "high 10" and push against each other. This provides good resistance for his upper body.

Interoception

This one is a bit trickier. To refresh your memory, the interoceptive sense comprises the signals your child receives from his internal organs and systems. His heart rate may be irregular, he may always feel thirsty or never hungry, his moods may swing wildly, or maybe he's extremely affected by temperature. Your child may experience difficulty regulating his internal temperature or recognizing the need to use the bathroom. It is difficult to target the interoceptive system specifically, but as a therapist, I have found that when you approach a child's entire sensory systems with a comprehensive approach, you will see results in this area, as well.

Fine-Motor Skills

There are many fine-motor activities you can try. A good one is squeezing miniature clothespins open and placing them onto the sides of a piece of paper. Using a hole-puncher to punch holes out of paper is always a fun activity for kids. You can also have your child string beads and make jewelry. Each of these activities assists with hand strengthening, finger dexterity, bilateral coordination, and eye-hand coordination. When you have to use both sides of your body together to complete an activity, such as stringing beads or catching a ball, this involves the use of bilateral coordination and eye-hand coordination, working in tandem. When children pick up small objects, like beads, they use what is called a "pincer grasp." This grasp should be evident around the age of 20 months.

For kids who are just learning to string beads, placing the beads onto a pipe cleaner can make it easier and reduce frustration.

The cotton ball "grabber" activity is fun because a cotton ball is light enough for everyone to pick up with the "grabbers" (tongs) and place into a bowl (Figure 7). It teaches a child how to manipulate

Figure 7. Cotton ball "grabber" activity (with tongs).

the "grabbers" while using eye-hand coordination to carry the cotton ball over and drop it into the bowl. You may also use beanbags that are slightly heavier and will make your child work a little harder. It requires more hand strength to pick up the beanbag with the grabber.

Making "flubber" can be a good time. Here's how to do it!

You'll need:

- ½ cup Elmer's Glue
- ⅓ cup warm water
- 1 teaspoon Borax
- ⅓ cup warm water
- food coloring (if desired)
- zipper storage bag
- small bowl
- spoon

Mix the glue, ⅓ cup warm water, and food coloring in a small bowl to make a glue solution. In a medium zipper storage bag, mix the Borax and ⅓ cup warm water to make a Borax solution. Pour the glue solution into the baggie of Borax solution. Gently squash the two together.

When the two solutions are all mixed together, you can take the flubber out and play with it in a bowl or on a covered table. Make sure you do not get this on your clothes!

When you make the flubber, you can have your child squeeze the glue into a cup or bowl. He may need to use two hands, which will strengthen the muscles in his hands, forearms, and even shoulders. When your child participates in creating things, it can motivate him to try things he usually won't, like touching sticky things or doing fine-motor activities. If you make it fun for him, he may not realize he's doing work at the same time.

Dropping food coloring into the bowl of glue solution is a good activity for your child to do, as he must grade his movements, meaning he has to be very gentle and have good hand and arm control to squeeze the dropper with just enough force—but not too much—to make the food coloring come out in individual drops.

Some kids enjoy feeling therapy goo like flubber on their hands. Kids that are tactile defensive will have a difficult time putting their hands into such a messy texture. One alternative is placing plastic bags or gloves over your child's hands so the goo doesn't actually touch his skin.

When you're making the goo, you can have a race when you squeeze out the glue to see who gets done first. It's good for your child to hold his arm in space for that length of time. You can work on fine-motor and visual-perceptual skills by having your child stand up and throw the therapy goo into a bucket to work on balance and trunk strengthening.

CHAPTER TEN

Sensory Therapies

Therapy Etiquette

Yes, parents, there are rules when it comes to doing therapy, and you need to learn them and follow them. Your child's therapists are there to help her, so let them do their job for her benefit.

Your therapist does not conjure up magic. Although it feels like it at times, because he or she can get your child to do things that you cannot, do not expect your therapist to wave a magic wand and "fix" your child's issues overnight.

Work out a time to talk to your therapists about your child's progress. Have all your questions ready, and use the last 10 minutes of your session to have a dialogue. You expect your therapist to come to therapy prepared, and the same is expected of you. If you have questions, write them down and be prepared. Do not send random e-mails at 3 o'clock in the morning and expect your therapist to be on call.

Don't routinely cancel appointments. If you'd like your therapist to keep appointments with your child, then you need to keep yours. It's a matter of mutual respect. If you find that your therapist is cancelling and rescheduling on you too often, perhaps it's time to find someone with a more stable schedule.

Ask your therapist for homework to do with your child. We cannot stress enough how important it is to work with your therapist. You spend a great deal of time with your child outside of therapy, and you can use that time to help your child with particular goals and tasks. If you don't understand what your therapist wants you to work on, it's okay to ask. For example, if you're not sure why she wants you to have your child play with play dough, ask. It could be that rolling out the dough works the muscles up your child's arms, shoulders, and back, which will help with handwriting. Often, there is a method behind the madness and it will become clear once your therapist communicates the theory.

Ask your therapist for books to read and videos to watch. Ply your therapist for anything that will help you understand what he or she is working on and how you can contribute. You will not become an OT by reading a book about occupational therapy, but it will help you understand and know your child better if he is working with an OT.

Therapy Expectations

As with all therapies, there should be expectations. We believe it's best to talk to your therapists about goals and timelines to keep your child's progress in check. Is tying shoelaces a task that your child may accomplish in 6 weeks? Could writing a full sentence with the proper pincer grasp take 8 months? Or is this a task that your child might not ever fully master? Sometimes the therapy goal is about quality of life and increasing your child's comfort level.

Sometimes you can tell when your child is no longer advancing with a particular therapy or even therapist. Has your child outgrown Applied Behavioral Analysis? Is your child no longer interested in music therapy? Maybe it's time to try something new. Please don't take this to mean you have to cram your child's schedule with new therapies. But, if your child has reached a plateau, it might be time for a change of scenery.

Next, we'd like to talk about realistic and unrealistic expectations. There are parents who think that therapists are supposed to "fix" their kids in the 50 minutes or less they see each other each week. And then there are those parents who mistake the therapist for a babysitter, whose job it is to visit with their child once a week and produce no results. Both are incorrect.

When you talk to your therapist about what he or she is working on with your child and you ask for homework, make sure you have realistic expectations for your child's progress. Ask about how many weeks or months it may take to master a particular skill. What types of indications should you look for at home, and what types of things should you not pay any attention to? With realistic boundaries, you set both yourself and your child up for success.

If you want to see your child make life-changing advancements after only 1 week of therapy, then you need a reality check. Don't be disappointed if your child doesn't make great strides in the very beginning. By having realistic expectations, you will take the extreme pressure off your child so she can master her task(s) without adding unnecessary stress.

On the other end of the spectrum, some parents may need to raise their expectations somewhat. I have found that therapists are remarkable at raising the bar and finding things that kids can do, to their parents' disbelief. So, your child can't talk—but maybe she can read and learn to type. Or, perhaps your child is unable to jump with both feet off the ground, but your therapist is able to get her to hop. Since your therapist is not your child's caretaker, he or she can often gauge from a more objective viewpoint what your child cannot do versus what your child will not do.

Therapy Burnout

It can be hard when a therapist exits your child's life, but therapist burnout is real, and it happens from time to time. Either a therapist decides to quit therapy altogether and needs to move on to a different career, or perhaps he or she doesn't fit in to your family's needs any longer. A therapist breakup can be tough, but know that sometimes it's necessary, and your family will make it through this change like you do so many others. Make sure to talk to your child about any therapist who is exiting her life, especially if it's a sudden departure and the two were close. You don't want your child to feel that she was the cause of any therapist breakup, and maybe you can help provide the positive closure that she may need.

Now, let's jump into some of the wonderful therapies available for your youngster!

Occupational Therapy

As an OT, I see children every day that have received a diagnosis of SPD, autism, Down syndrome, cerebral palsy, attention-deficit/hyperactivity disorder (ADHD), developmental delays, and many other disabilities.

Occupational therapy can be a very complex profession, as we see so many different types of patients and can treat patients from birth all the way up to old age. So, sometimes it can be hard to understand when your child may need occupational therapy.

If your child received a diagnosis of autism spectrum disorder, SPD, ADHD, or any other developmental disability, she probably needs outpatient or clinic-based occupational therapy. Your school and early-intervention programs can also provide services, but they can only address what is relevant from an educational standpoint. Most children in these programs really need more intensive therapy according to a medically based model, in addition to what the education model can provide. Many times, your insurance will cover outpatient services for your child. Clinical occupational therapy should be administered by a highly trained therapist who specializes in a sensory-integration approach and focuses on relationship and engagement.

Service Animals, Therapy Animals, and Companion Animals

As an OT, I have taken my dog, Frankie, through the Delta Society Pet Partner training, and she is a certified therapy dog. She actually goes with me to the clinic where I work in Colorado, and she works with the children there. She does more than a typical therapy dog does and will allow the children to take her through an obstacle course. She runs through tunnels, jumps through suspended tire swings, and climbs onto platform swings to swing with the kids (Figure 8). She also helps teach children how to keep their bodies calm and work on their arousal level. Frankie is very patient and loving with even the younger children, and she allows them to pet her and lay on her. It is beneficial for children and adults to be around these types of dogs, which are well trained for emotional regulation and sensory input. It makes therapy even more fun!

Therapy animals are animals that are trained to serve a few different purposes. Some therapy animals and dogs are trained through a national society to work with a pet partner and visit hospitals, skilled nursing facilities, and schools. They are used to hone social skills in children, enhance the positive

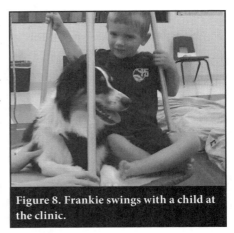

Figure 8. Frankie swings with a child at the clinic.

environment of a skilled nursing facility, visit the sick in the hospital, and more. If you'd like to train your dog as a therapy dog, check out *www.deltasociety.org* and *www.tdi-dog.org.*

Service animals, on the other hand, are highly trained animals (typically dogs) that assist people with disabilities. These dogs and animals are not pets. Two examples are guide animals, which are trained to guide the blind, and hearing animals, which help those who are hearing impaired. Other types of service animals might assist someone in a wheelchair. These service animals are allowed to go anywhere a disabled person goes, including airplanes, restaurants, and stores. To look up the minimum standards for service animals, go to *www.deltasociety.org* and look under "Service Animal Basics."

In September 2010, the Civil Rights Division of the U.S. Department of Justice redefined a service animal as any dog that is specially trained to work or perform certain tasks to assist an individual with a disability. This includes physical, sensory, psychiatric, intellectual, mental, and other disabilities.[20]

Autism dogs are trained by a specific facility to work with children who have autism or behavioral issues. These dogs are trained to be tethered to a child with autism. If the child tries to run off, the animal will lie down to keep the child from getting away. The dog can also lie on top of the child to help calm her down in the event of a tantrum or meltdown. There are other things that these autism dogs are trained to do, and as a result, they can be very beneficial for the right family. Because they are so well trained, these dogs are very expensive. You can look into autism dogs at *www.autismservicedogsofamerica.com*, a company based out of Oregon, as well as *www.autism.wilderwood.org*, out of Tennessee. There are other resources online as well, if you search for "autism dogs."

Companion dogs and animals do not do any work, but they do provide companionship for a person and/or a family. They do not have rights like a service dog to be in stores, airports, or restaurants. These dogs can be trained by an outside facility or by the owner. There are some companion dogs that can help provide comfort to an elderly person or someone who is disabled, but they are not always trained to complete specific jobs for them like a service dog would. One resource based out of Iowa is *www.disabilityassistancedogs.org*. Studies have shown that people with dogs tend to live healthier, longer, more fulfilling and active lives.

No matter what, when you look into getting a pet for your family, you need to take many things into consideration:

- Do you have time to spend with an animal—training it, exercising it, and loving it?
- Do you have the financial resources to take care of a pet?
- Is the animal a good fit for your family? If you have children, would it be a good pet for children?
- If you are thinking about choosing a dog that you would like to become a therapy or companion dog, or just a pet for your family, you want to test the dog's temperament first to make sure it is not going to be too aggressive.

- A good resource is *The Art of Raising a Puppy*. In the back of that book is advice on testing a puppy for temperament.
- You also want to look into the breed of dog you're considering to find out how well that breed interacts with kids and families. How easily is that breed trained? Also, does that breed get along with other animals, if you have any?
- If you want to rescue a dog from the shelter, please make sure you really look at all the aspects of the animal. Just because an animal looks cute in that cage does not mean you need to bring it home to your house, where you've got toddlers running around.
- Many people can be either slightly or severely allergic to dogs. Not to worry—there are many breeds of hypoallergenic dogs out there! You do have options.
- Make sure you do your homework before bringing home any sort of animal, even if it's a cat, a bird, or a hamster.

Sometimes you can find therapists, like myself, who have a trained therapy dog that will work with your child in a therapy setting to help her. Some therapists are trained in animal-assisted therapy, where the therapist and the animal are taken through more advanced training to learn how to employ the animal appropriately in therapeutic settings. Visit *www.deltasociety.org* and look under "Animal Assisted Therapy" for more information.

If children are frightened of dogs, you can slowly introduce them to a therapy dog or another highly trained dog that you know is tolerant of children. I will sometimes let a child look at Frankie through the window first, or she can stand back and watch her parent pet Frankie. Frankie will lie down on the floor in a passive position and wait for the child to approach her when she is ready. Sometimes children are fearful of a dog's head or face and would rather begin petting the dog on the back, close to the tail. Another good way to break the ice with a child is by having the dog perform some tricks or having the dog shake the child's hand. If the kids are up for it, I have them give Frankie a treat. She is very gentle when she takes it out of their fingers. Sometimes it takes several meetings before a child is comfortable working with her, but there is no rush. I would rather have a child come around on her own time, than force her to experience something that will send her into fight-or-flight mode.

Aquatic Therapy

Swimming is excellent for body awareness. In general, swimming provides great proprioception and vestibular input to the body. The resistance the water provides creates an increased awareness of the body and how it moves. Pushing off of the wall provides even more pressure. Aquatic therapy increases range of motion, endurance, strengthening, flexibility, and cardiovascular function. It also increases respiration. Bending to the sides while swimming helps inflate individual lobes of the lungs.

During aquatic therapy, the pool should be heated to temperatures between 86 and 96 degrees. The body's passive range of motion is enhanced by the warmth of the water. The heated water also promotes inhibition of spastic muscles. The water's buoyancy virtually eliminates the effects of gravity. It supports 90% of the body's weight, for reduced impact and greater flexibility. Water also acts as a cushion for weight-bearing joints and reduces the stress on muscles, tendons, and ligaments.

Your child may need to wear a life vest when she first gets in the pool, and that is okay. If she's fearful of the water, let her take her time. With a child that's new to the water, allow her to use goggles if she prefers, so she doesn't get water in her eyes. Nose plugs may be used, as well. As a child develops the ability to move and enjoy the water, there is a definite improvement in her self-awareness and self-esteem.

Sometimes, kids need to watch you do an activity first so they can model you. You may also use picture cards to show a child what you expect of her; however, if you use picture cards for swimming, the cards should be laminated or waterproofed first.

Alerting the body with activities like blowing bubbles in the pool with a straw can help "wake up" the brain and increase your child's attention and awareness. This is an activity that strengthens oral-motor abilities and helps to focus your child. It is nice to see the bubbles in the water to get some visual feedback.

Having your child walk around the pool and jump in at a designated area will help her learn to follow directions and wait for her turn. This also assists with impulse control. Some children respond well to hand signals, in addition to verbal instruction.

Working with a ball in the pool is great for visual-motor skills and hand-eye coordination. A beach ball is nice because it is light and will fly longer and give your child an extra second or two to process how to catch the ball when you toss it to her. You can also push the ball underwater. One way to give children feedback in their upper body is to have them push dumbbells in the water. This also strengthens their shoulders, which will come in handy for swimming, writing, climbing, and other fine-motor tasks. Having a child hold on to the wall of the pool while kicking strengthens both the upper and lower extremities.

Floating helps calm and is a good tool to use when transitioning to different parts of the pool. Floating is also a nice way to relax the body when a child is too stimulated because a large portion of her body is underwater.

A final note about swimming: Never allow your child to swim without adult supervision. At least one adult at the pool should know cardiopulmonary resuscitation, or CPR. Keep all pool chemicals locked away. Before attempting any aquatic therapy, you must get approval from your doctor.

Auditory Integration Training

We spoke with Auditory Integration Training (AIT) specialist Khymberleigh Herwill-Levin about what AIT is and what it's for. According to Khymberleigh, AIT is a type of auditory therapy for children who are not reaching their full educational and social potential. Children with auditory processing disorder have "perfectly functioning" ears but a faulty "relay station." This means that what they hear is delayed and interfered with on the way to the brain, where the sound is processed (sorted).

Auditory processing disorder makes it difficult for the brain to modulate sound. Sometimes, a person's auditory processing abilities can be so dysfunctional that ordinary sounds seem acutely uncomfortable. Hyperacusis, or overresponsive auditory processing, often affects those with better-than-average hearing. In a classroom situation, for instance, a child may not be able to stay focused and process the teacher's voice without also hearing the scuffling of feet, whispering, birds singing outside, lawn-mowing in the distance, or soccer being played nearby. Some children have such acute auditory sensitivity that they can hear their own heart beating or even that of their peers. Their breathing and their peers' breathing can be so loud for them that they are unable to focus on anything else. This can cause a child to become irritable and cranky and act aggressively and/or in an inappropriate manner.

Just because a child can hear "within normal limits" does not mean that he or she has good processing abilities. Even a slight hearing loss will affect a child far more than it would an adult, because the child is still learning about his environment and gaining life skills through listening. Audiologists, who test hearing, often find that children have a 5-dB to 15-dB hearing loss in certain frequencies. This is considered "hearing within normal limits." A young child needs a good hearing mechanism that will deliver clear sounds to facilitate healthy auditory processing. But, this does not mean that adults are not also affected.

The principle behind AIT is simple. In the auditory system, concise zones exist from the eardrum to the brain, which conduct both low- and high-pitched tones. If these zones are stimulated by programmed alternating sounds, it is believed that the auditory cortex in the brain reorganizes. The treatment gives the ear an aerobic workout, as it exer-

Figure 9. Jackie's son Odin receives Auditory Integration Therapy.

cises and strengthens the muscles that control the small bones found in the middle ear. It thereby retrains the ear's response to sound, which helps prevent sensory overload (Figure 9).

The Berard method of AIT is a technique that stimulates the brain's neural pathways with electronically altered music to help the hearing mechanism transmit sound more efficiently. The music is administered for an hour a day (in two half-hour sessions per day), for 10 consecutive days. In some cases, the treatment needs to be repeated 5 to 10 months later. AIT can improve a wide range of problems, such as allergies, irritability, hyperactivity, attention-deficit disorder, ADHD, speech defects, hypersensitive hearing, central auditory processing disorder, underresponsive processing, pervasive developmental delay, and autism.

Some side effects can occur after each session, such as an increase in appetite, headaches, nausea, irritability, and extreme fatigue. Physical and/or behavioral side effects have been experienced by many participants, and these are considered a sign of positive change. The side effects cease as the body adjusts to the new, incoming stimuli. No side effect has lasted permanently. All participants are monitored by a Berard-trained AIT practitioner, and children can have a parent or guardian sit with them during each session.

You can read more about AIT and Khymberleigh Herwill-Levin at *www.ait1st.com.*

Integrated Listening Systems

Integrated Listening Systems (iLs) is a multisensory program that improves brain function. It is an enjoyable activity or "exercise" that can be customized for all ages and skill levels for implementation in the clinic, at school, or at home.

iLs can influence a person's sense of balance, vision, hearing, motor skills, coordination, behavior, and emotional regulation. As a result, it can assist with a number of deficits, including auditory processing disorder, learning disabilities, reading difficulties, attention and regulation, SPD, and speech and language delays.

With iLs, a child wears headphones that are connected to an iPod he wears in a backpack while he plays in the gym for therapy, or he wears the headphones at home while participating in movement activities. There are many listening programs on the market, and as an OT, I see great benefits from this particular program for multiple reasons.

Q&A on iLs with Lindsay Fogerty, MS, OTR

Lindsay Fogerty MS, OTR, began her relationship with the STAR Center in 2006 when she volunteered as an aide. There, she furthered her understanding of SPD and her passion for working with children who have the disorder. She received her masters in occupational therapy from Tufts University, where her emphasis was working with children. Lindsay has training and experience with the "Alert Program" and "MORE: Integrating the Mouth with Sensory and Postural Functions," as well as extensive training in iLs.

Q: Why is iLs beneficial for children?
A: The iLs program offers a variety of options to fit the needs of the children I treat at the STAR Center. It is beneficial for targeting different areas of the brain through a variety of body systems, including the auditory, vestibular, and visual systems. The improvements in coordination, balance, and auditory processing are often the most immediate of the changes we see in children after they start an iLs program. However, the emotional regulation and behavioral improvements are often profound. Children that used to cry or anger easily often appear to "feel better in their own skin" after completing an iLs program. For a child with speech difficulties, iLs is powerful for helping the child hear sounds in a more meaningful way. It activates the trigeminal nerve (which contains both sensory and motor fibers), so the child knows where her mouth is and can use it in a way she might not have before. The child is able to hear her own voice in an integral way, through her headphones and bone conduction.

Overall, the benefits and changes we see in children that use iLs during occupational therapy occur in half the time they would with therapy alone.

Q: How can iLs help adults?
A: I completed an iLs program myself, and it boosted my energy level and soothed my level of irritability. At the STAR Center, many parents find it beneficial to complete a program either during or after their child completes treatment. The stress and demands of parenting a child with a disability or disorder are unparalleled. iLs provides the calming, grounding relaxation that adults need to decrease their anxiety level and improve their ability to sleep.

Q: When do you decide to use iLs with children with sensory issues?
A: In my experience, almost every child with sensory issues benefits

from iLs. After completing the program, children with modulation difficulties (especially children that are overresponsive) often have a greater tolerance for movement, tactile input, and auditory input. The iLs program stimulates the vagus nerve, which conducts sensory messages about the internal organs. Thus, iLs provides activation of the parasympathetic system. This helps children who operate primarily from fight-or-flight mode become more organized and calm. I find it to be a jumping-off point for a child to be able to take more risks when it comes to motor and social development. Children with postural disorder develop better coordination and balance, which allows them to do more with their bodies in play. With tactile discrimination, for example, children's tactile systems become more organized, and they are able to better understand the subtleties of what they feel. Some children are not able to handle the intensity of therapy with the additional sensory input; however, I recommend that these children complete a program either before or after their intensive therapy. Like any program, there are contraindications, and the program is not recommended for all children.

Q: *What makes iLs different from other listening therapies?*
A: The iLs treatment is unique because it engages a variety of sensory systems in tandem. In addition, iLs has "at home" programs that are easy to use and customize. The whole family is able to participate in a program, if desired, and the children we treat at the STAR Center are able to continue to "boost" the gains they made during their intensive therapy. The bone conduction and quality of the music is unique to iLs. For children that typically come to the STAR Center for the treatment of significant sensory issues, iLs allows them to take more time moving through the filtration and intensity of music. This allows their nervous systems

to make adaptations to be able to benefit from the filtration and lays a strong foundation for treatment. Other programs can be intense and not comfortable for the listener. With iLs, each session is designed to address specific areas of concern and ends with a calming and grounding track, leaving the child in a more regulated state. iLs also incorporates vocal chant, which no other program does. This can be influential for slowing down a child's heart rate and providing a relaxing effect.

Q: What do you do for a child that won't wear the headphones?
A: Younger children and/or those who are overresponsive may have trouble with this. A child may not like anything touching her head, so we try to build her tolerance slowly. We might have her wear dress-up hats or sunglasses or put silly things on her head during playtime. Sometimes, families hook up big, comfy headphones to the TV and allow the child to watch her favorite show—if she wears the headphones to listen to the sound. Some children are just not ready yet, and after a round of therapy, they may begin to tolerate the headphones afterward. Sometimes if they see other children wearing them, or their parents try them on, they are more open to it. They could try the headphones on even for just a few minutes at a time, with no sound coming out, during playtime to increase their ability to tolerate the feeling of the headphones.

Which Auditory Treatment Is Best?

When it comes to determining which auditory program might be best for your child, we wanted to bring in an expert opinion. We talked to Randall Redfield, cofounder and CEO of iLs, to see what the differences are between AIT, iLs, and the Therapeutic Listening program. Here is what he had to say.

Q&A on Listening Therapies with Randall Redfield

Q: How is iLs different from AIT?

A: The iLs program is different from AIT in every aspect, from its underlying premises to its content, structure, and hardware:

- *Therapeutic approach:* iLs is a multisensory approach that combines sound and movement, as well as receptive and expressive language. AIT's method involves a receptive auditory program only.

- *Visual, vestibular, and balance activities:* iLs uses visual, vestibular, and balance input simultaneously with sound to further regulation, motor skills, and language integration.

- *Music selection and processing methods:* iLs processes classical music by using audio techniques, such as filtration and gating—methods that are unrelated to AIT's Digital Audio Aerobics, or DAA, machine.

- *Sound delivery:* iLs is delivered via air and bone conduction, which is how we normally hear ourselves speak. AIT is delivered via air conduction only.

- *Hardware/equipment:* The iLs audio program is delivered via an iPod; AIT's program is delivered via the DAA machine.

- *Program structure:* iLs has structured programs that are 40-60 hours in length. The AIT programs are 10 hours each.

- *Complementary therapy:* iLs is used in conjunction with other therapies, such as occupational therapy, physical and speech therapy, working with a psychologist, and working with educators in school settings. iLs makes no claims about cures and but emphasizes its complementary nature. AIT is said to be exclusive and prohibits the use of other listening programs after the use of AIT.

Q: How does iLs differ from the Therapeutic Listening program?

We receive a lot of feedback regarding Therapeutic Listening from the therapists we train, as most OTs that specialize in a sensory-based approach have trained in it. The two programs could be considered "complementary," but most therapists use one or the other. Both are auditory training programs, but iLs is different in a few specific ways:

1. *Bone conduction:* This way of delivering sound stimulates the vestibular system. It is arguably the most important element of listening therapy, and it's one that especially works with a lot of sensory issues.

2. *Combination of sound and movement:* iLs combines specific vestibular and visual-tracking activities with the auditory program. Of course, OTs have their own sensory regimen, but many incorporate iLs activities into their OT gym. iLs makes it easy for parents who are doing supplementary therapy at home to do a multisensory program with their child.

3. *Technology:* With iLs, we find that iPods are a better form of delivery than playing CDs or disks. You can't scratch or lose the recordings, and they don't skip during programs. Therapeutic Listening now has a non-CD product, but it compresses the music, so the quality is less than that of a CD.

4. *Music quality:* A consistent observation from users is that iLs music is high quality, is never abrasive, and remains pleasant throughout the various levels of filtration and processing.

5. *Customization:* We are very encouraged by the comparative feedback we receive with regard to the organization, quality, and customizing aspects of our program.

6. *Interactive language program:* This iLs program is used by many OTs, as well as by educators and speech-language pathologists. To my knowledge, Therapeutic Listening does

not work on specific aspects of auditory processing with an express program.

Comparisons aside, I think it is safe to say that the main reason we get the results we do is that we combine a few elements that work well together: a quality bone-conduction system, program designs that are easy to use and customize for different clients' needs, and effective technology.

You can read more about iLs at *www.integratedlistending systems.com*.

Massage Therapy

Massage can be beneficial for all of us—parents included. Children can benefit from massage, as long as it is performed correctly by someone who is trained and experienced in massaging children. If a child likes being touched, massage can help calm him down when he is stressed, overresponsive, or anxious. Massage provides input through the tactile system, offering deep pressure through the proprioceptors in the body and conducting positive energy from the massager to the child. This can be very beneficial.

I have taken a course in craniosacral therapy, and it was very interesting. I felt like I learned a lot about the body and how it works. There is some controversy around craniosacral therapy for children and adults, but if it is something that interests you, visit *www.upledger.com* for more information. Other therapists and families have found success in a practice called Quigong, for children with autism and SPD. Please visit *www. qsti.org* to learn more.

Q&A with Abbie Logwood, Massage Therapist

Abbie Logwood has been a nationally and state-certified massage therapist since 2001. Abbie worked for many years as a counselor for at-risk teenagers and women in a psychiatric residential setting. She has recently continued her massage education with a focus on trauma therapy.

Q: *Who can benefit from massage?*
A: Anyone who needs to relax and release tension can benefit from a massage. There are many wonderful and different types of massage techniques that an individual can receive to assist with this process.

Q: *Does massage therapy have to be deep to be effective?*
A: No. A massage therapist who is well educated in many different methods can provide a lighter massage and a slower pace, which can also be quite effective. I even know of one therapist who is no longer physically able to do deep-massage work. She told her regular clients she would continue to work with them, but it would be with a lighter touch. She said that even the most serious of her deep-tissue clients stayed with her and actually enjoy the benefits of using less pressure.

Q: *What should parents do to prepare themselves and/or their children for a massage?*
A: I think the most important preparation for a massage, especially a first massage, is for you to feel completely comfortable with your therapist. A child needs to feel safe with a therapist. Go to someone you like, who is licensed and knowledgeable and who will listen to your concerns and be patient. Once you are lying on the table and the massage has begun, if at any time you feel uncomfortable with the pressure or technique you are receiving, be sure to tell your

therapist. Remember, this is your massage to enjoy! It is better not to have a massage on a full stomach, so refrain from eating right before your session.

Q: *What results have you seen with craniosacral massage?*
A: This is one of the most delicate massage techniques that I perform, and it involves working primarily with the rhythm or waves of the cerebrospinal fluid throughout the body. Palpating and applying a light touch at specific points on the body appears to put many clients in a comfort zone that they cannot otherwise achieve through a regular full-body massage. The clients that request a craniosacral session prefer this therapy over other "standard" types of full-body massages, and those who receive it often fall asleep on the table during a session.

Q: *Is there anything you want people to know about massage?*
A: I think massage is one of the most natural healing experiences we can give to ourselves and to each other. The moment you recline on the table, you often sense a profound awareness of a connection between your mind and body, and this can be the beginning to understanding and achieving a well-balanced lifestyle.

Yoga for Children

Yoga seems to be the new craze for kids. Yoga is about union and oneness, and it doesn't require any "doing" to experience it. "It is what you are." Yoga is great because it allows children to grade the force of their movements. Slowly moving into yoga poses does not push their muscles into full extension, so they're able to increase their muscle strength while cognitively becoming aware of where their body is in space.

Yoga can improve gross- and fine-motor strength, breath support, concentration, and even communication skills. We talked with an OT who is also a yoga instructor, and she helped us realize that there are specific things you need to look for in a yoga class—especially one for your child.

There are different types of yoga practices. A few of them are Anusara yoga (which means "flowing with Grace," "flowing with Nature," and following your heart), Kirtan yoga (the spirit of chanting), Karma yoga (the discipline of action), and Raja yoga (the "royal union"). There are many more.

When looking for a yoga class for your child, make sure you look for a class that:

- Has relaxation built into the program for the younger kids. It is important to teach children how to relax, as we are constantly on the go and need to learn how to slow down.
- Has meditation for the older kids.
- Focuses on the alignment of body postures. We want to make sure that children's bodies are being protected and moved in ways that will not cause injury.
- Has an instructor who is well trained in anatomy and alignment.
- Interests your child! This is important because we can't force our children to participate in something they don't want to do.
- Is playful and theme based and tells a story through movement.
- Is more upbeat and fun and geared toward kids.
- Focuses on breathing.

One example of how to teach children to breathe is by using the Hoberman Mini Sphere ball (Figure 10). As the ball opens, we take a deep breath in, and as it slowly closes, we blow the air out.

You can also have kids hold a tissue up to their noses and practice slowly moving the tissue with their breath.

The benefits of yoga are many and include the following:

- Inverted postures, where the head is below the heart, increase blood flow and begin to clear the lymphatic system.
- Yoga helps to build strength and body tone.
- It helps move energy all around and throughout the body.
- It increases a person's overall state of health.
- It increases coordination, flexibility, and the ability to relax.
- Yoga helps build self-confidence in children.
- It promotes body awareness.
- It's an activity that kids of all abilities and developmental levels can do.

You can check out our DVD, "Yoga for Children with Special Needs," to learn more. The DVD features yoga instructor Aras Baskauskas, who takes children through a yoga routine while Britt makes suggestions regarding your child's specific special needs.

Figure 10. The Hoberman Mini Sphere can be useful for teaching children how to breathe slowly, as the sphere opens and closes. It's available at *www.hoberman.com*.

SENSORY PARENTING: THE ELEMENTARY YEARS

CHAPTER ELEVEN

SPD and Special Needs

The latest research studies show that about 90% of children with autism spectrum disorder manifest some degree of sensory-processing dysfunction.[21] It is hypothesized that significantly fewer kids diagnosed with SPD also have autism spectrum disorder, but more research needs to be done to confirm this. The two disorders are not one and the same.

Author Chantal Sicile-Kira interviewed autistic adults and teenagers of different ability levels for her book, *Autism Life Skills*. Chantal reports that although SPD is not considered a qualifying characteristic for a diagnosis of autism, she has yet to meet a person on the autism spectrum who does not have sensory challenges. Most of them indicated that their number-one difficulty is sensory-processing challenges, regardless of where they are on the spectrum.[22]

The Diagnostic and Statistical Manual of Mental Disorders is currently undergoing adjustments to the diagnostic criteria for autism. The newly proposed guidelines are scheduled to include over- and underresponsivity to sensory input or an unusual interest in the sensory aspects of one's environment. This can mean an indifference to pain, heat, or cold, adverse responses to specific sounds or textures, excessive smelling or touching of objects, and fascination with lights or spinning objects. Symptoms like these serve to limit and impair a child's everyday ability to function.

For more discussion about possible signs of autism, please review Appendix D. In this Appendix, we have also included material from our first book about coexisting conditions that children with sensory sensitivities may have.

How to Know If Your Child Has Autism or SPD

The main difference between autism and SPD is that children with autism typically do not have the inner drive to want to share experiences with others. Children who do not meet all the diagnostic criteria for autism but show signs of sensory sensitivities that impede their ability to function in daily life may have SPD. Sometimes it is very difficult to tell whether your child has autism or SPD, and it takes a trained professional that is well versed in both disorders to know the difference. Many cases are misdiagnosed, and we want to make sure you get the right diagnosis for your child. There are times when families run into issues with their insurance coverage, and we have seen families that want the autism diagnosis so they can get services. We try to discourage mislabeling your child's condition. Ultimately, a therapist treats the symptoms and not the diagnosis. If you are trying to get services through your school, it can be difficult to have your child qualify with a diagnosis of SPD. But, if it is affecting his ability to learn and participate in his education, then you should pursue the accommodations your child needs.

SPD versus Attention-Deficit Disorder and ADHD

How do you know if your child has SPD, an attention-deficit disorder, or both? Well, it depends on your child's characteristics and behaviors. Sometimes, it seems like a child is "spacing out" or not paying attention in class, when really he is on "sensory overload" and is trying to tune out the overwhelming stimuli. There are also times when a child appears to be "bouncing off the walls" and is unable to sit still and focus on a task, but he could be a sensory craver and need movement to maintain his arousal level and be able to focus. Again, it takes a trained professional that understands both diagnoses so he or she can assign an accurate diagnosis. Sometimes a child receives a diagnosis of attention-deficit disorder or ADHD, and the medication he is given doesn't work. Maybe he has tried several medications, and none of them seems to have any effect. This child may get better results from sensory therapy and no ADHD medications. If so, this kiddo may actually have SPD and not ADHD.

Research studies have been conducted at the STAR Center in Greenwood Village, Colorado, to help determine the difference between SPD and ADHD. According to Miller et al, children with ADHD are impulsive, inattentive, and hyperactive, while children with sensory modulation disorder (one subtype of SPD) have difficulty responding adaptively to daily sensory experiences."[23] The children in the study were exposed to various stimuli, while their responses were measured.

For instance, a feather was brushed gently against a child's cheek, or a child's chair was tipped backward suddenly. The stimulus was presented to the children several times, and the responses were measured each time through what is called *electrodermal response* and were recorded with a computer program. The findings of the research study indicated that children with ADHD habituated to the stimuli (or got used to them), while children with sensory modulation disorder continued to show an intense response to the stimuli. This means that children with ADHD can tune out a stimuli and focus on a task, but children with sensory modulation disorder or overresponsivity cannot, because each time their bodies experience the stimuli, they go into fight, flight, or freeze mode.

For more specifics about this research study, please visit *www. spdfoundation.net* and look for it under the "Research" tab.

Q&A with Alma Short on Raising a Child with Autism

Alma Short lives in a small farming community and has two sons, one of whom received a diagnosis of autism. We asked Alma what it was like to have a child with autism.

Alma and Aidan

We were curious about whether her struggles were different than those of us who live in a city where services for our children are readily available.

Q: When did your son receive a diagnosis of autism?
A: When he was 3 years old. We had to drive 185 miles to Phoenix to get Aidan evaluated. On that day, my life completely changed. In many ways, he seemed like a typically developing baby, and everyone in my family thought I was insane for taking him to be evaluated. But, I followed my gut instincts. I felt I had waited too long and wasted too much time taking him to local doctors, who told me that he was fine and just a little "behind" developmentally. Aidan made no eye contact. I had heard about autism, but I didn't really know much about it. No one in my family or my husband's family had it. I wasn't prepared at all. I just knew something was wrong and that Aidan had problems with his stomach, so I refused to give up. I got a referral and took him to Phoenix. I met with a neurologist, and the evaluation took a few hours. Before I left, the neurologist said the words "autism" and "severe" and "ADHD." I immediately went into a funk. I hadn't realized that I was going to walk out of there with a diagnosis! The neurologist gave me a plan, including therapies and developmental preschool, but I wasn't really given any other information or studies on biomedical options. The neurologist was very discouraging about diets and other types of treatments.

The next morning, I cried it out with my sister. She hugged me and said, "He's the same child he was before the diagnosis. This is happening to him, not to you." It was a slap on the face to me, but she was right. Just like that, my sister made me see that I was not a victim (which came in super handy later, when I had to handle the frustrations of not being able to do much to help him in our hometown). This was happening to Aidan, and all I knew was that I was going to do everything I could to help my child.

Q: Once you had the autism diagnosis, what did you do?
A: When I got home, I felt I had both family support and a plan.

I was ready and excited to get started with the therapies. That's when I realized I was going to have to travel to get treatment for Aidan. There were no services available in our town. It was extremely frustrating. I called everyone—hospitals, rehabilitation centers, and schools. I talked to teachers and begged for help for my son. I told my husband, "I'm going to leave you and move to Phoenix!" I didn't really want to, and I wouldn't have, but it was my instinct to move. The doctors in my hometown simply attributed Aidan's stomach problems to his autism.

My next step was contacting the state department about assessing Aidan's disabilities. They came and checked him out. Aidan qualified for services, but the problem was, there was a 2-year wait to get services anywhere in our area! So, I enrolled him in a developmental preschool. He got some services through the school, but not much, as there were too many kids and not enough professionals. I kept pursuing help. I visited more schools, even ones that weren't in our district. I was sure it was a matter of only one person taking pity on us.

Finally, one speech-language pathologist decided to give Aidan a chance. The speech therapist, whom I refer to as The Wonderful Miss Pilar, started working with Aidan right away and is still working with him. I'm so grateful for her. In the beginning, Aidan had echolalia (the echoing of words spoken by other people) and no other form of speech. He was unaware of me and had never called me "Mom."

We slowly integrated biomedical treatments and different diets, and, over time, we began to see results. Aidan began to progress.

Next, I contacted the state disability law department, because I had no idea what Aidan's rights were. In our small town, a lot of people are not educated about this topic, and the ones who are tend to be really busy. I felt that I was just listening to others tell me what was going to be done with Aidan at school. But, I discovered that if you find yourself listening to someone who isn't sure about what to do, then you need to know your stuff and speak up. No matter what, you have to be your child's biggest advocate. No one is going to hold your hand.

When it comes to my son, I can be pushy and aggressive, questioning everyone. One time, the school "lost" Aidan. Someone called the police because they saw a little kid running down the street by himself. The police found him, but Aidan couldn't talk to them. That was a very scary day. After that happened, I realized I had to be more on top of everything going on with my son. Educating myself about his rights has helped us out a lot along the way.

I went to an autism support group. I wanted a group with whom I could share information on resources. But, it turned out to be a pity party, which I just didn't have time for. The support group stopped having meetings, but I still exchange e-mails with other members of the group. If others hear about something important, they let the rest of us know. I find communication with other parents to be a great resource. Thanks to those e-mails, I have become aware of classes we can take and things I can do to advocate for Aidan. It's too bad, but many times, people don't show up to classes because they don't know the classes exist.

Q: How did you find the help you needed for your child?
A: I was very fortunate to be able to drive to a big city often and get training in Applied Behavioral Analysis. Also, I started looking into biomedical approaches there. For more than 3 years, I spent about 3 days a week in Phoenix to get Aidan as much therapy as possible. We did genetic testing and started chelation therapy in Phoenix, until Aidan was able to tell my husband and I that he didn't like it.

Q: What other therapies have you tried with Aidan?
A: We have tried a lot of different things. Changing his diet has been big. We did allergy testing and removed everything he was allergic to from his diet—mostly dairy. His stomach was always bloated. I remember watching him lean over the couch or on a ball to put pressure on his tummy. He had a big problem with yeast. At 6 years old, he was still not potty trained, and I couldn't take him to day care. Trying to get him to be social in public places was even more difficult. We tried the gluten-free/casein-free diet, since my husband insisted on it. It was really hard at first, having to cook everything in advance. We did notice that Aidan started talking more while he was on this diet, and we kept it up for 3 years. After talking to a doctor in California about Aidan not being able to use the bathroom, I decided to start a different diet. We did a very specific carbohydrate diet, and it was amazing, but it was also a very, very hard diet to follow. We had to make everything from scratch, but it was worth it because it helped Aidan's stomach so much. Within 2 weeks of starting the new diet, he started using the bathroom on his own. He no longer had to carry Pull-Ups in his backpack.

We continue to do speech therapy. We found a good OT who opened his own treatment center, but, sadly, the center didn't last long. I believe many people here don't have the resources to keep up with all these therapies and treatments.

We have tried play therapy and hippotherapy. I honestly don't know if these really helped Aidan, but he liked them and I took him whenever I could.

Hyperbaric oxygen therapy has been helpful for Aidan. This involves breathing pure oxygen in a pressurized room. He did 60 sessions in a rotation, twice a day for 30 days, and then we took time off.

Aidan also did AIT, twice a day for 10 days. The AIT was administered to a big group of people, so it may not have been as effective as it could have been. I would like for him to do it again. We did see some positive changes during AIT, and he was able to sit at a table and play a card game with the family for the very first time.

One of my favorite therapies is neurofeedback. I love it because I see results quickly! Aidan makes more eye contact and engages in activities for longer periods of time after neurofeedback. He gets into social stories more and no longer needs reminders or pictures to be able to function. I can get him to do simple tasks by himself, like getting dressed. His shoes, shirt, and shorts may not match, but it doesn't matter! He did it himself.

Currently, we are following Dr Amy Yasko's protocol. I dragged my husband to one of her conferences in Los Angeles, and he found it to be very interesting and is supportive of Aidan doing it. My husband has taken over the responsibility of handling all of Aidan's supplements.

Honestly, we have tried so many different things. I want to make sure I don't leave any rock unturned.

Q: What would you like to tell other parents of children with autism?
A: I really don't feel like I can give advice to anyone. All I have is my experience with Aidan.

One mistake I made was that I wanted to do everything right away. I started all kinds of things at the same time. I kept a journal of everything that was going on. But which therapy or supplement or medication worked? If I had to go back and do it all over again, I would introduce one thing at a time.

To parents who are new to autism, I would love to tell them to slow down and just take one day at a time. You don't have to always be running. I was so desperate and sleep deprived and felt so guilty for neglecting everybody else. Now, when I look back to the way I was 5 years ago, it seems silly because Aidan is wonderful and he's doing just fine. However, I don't know if I could follow my own advice to slow down if I had to go through it again.

To parents who live in places with limited services, I would say, yes, it is really hard living in a place where help is hard to get. More than likely, you are not alone, so don't give up hope. I've seen amazing changes in our town during the past 5 years. We still don't have much, but compared to when I started this journey, it is something. Caring parents who want more for their children have made all the difference. I've seen parents take it upon themselves to bring resources into our area from other places.

Q: What are your hopes and dreams for Aidan?
A: I dream of Aidan being independent one day. When his autism was first diagnosed, the doctor told me, "Your child is going to need care forever and will never drive a car." This did not give me much hope. Aidan is now 8. We still have a long way to go. I don't consider myself a crazy parent, thinking I'm going to completely cure my child of autism, but I do like to dream for my son. A dear friend whom I have met along this journey has gotten wonderful results with her own son, and she keeps me going. I know Aidan will keep making progress. I do know Aidan is always going to be a little quirky, but I see his potential, because he's a totally different child than when he first received a diagnosis.

I never thought of myself dying before, but now I do, because I'm responsible for this child with autism. So, I have to make sure he is independent one day. My life is not what I thought it would be like as a mother, but it is great. I have met wonderful people because of Aidan. Some of them have become our closest friends. I'm going to keep fighting for my child, and I will never take no for an answer.

In Closing

We hope that this book has provided you with some valuable information about your child's development and given you some insights on how to help your life together run more smoothly. As parents, we all work really hard to "keep our heads above water" at times. We hope that you now have some new tools in your toolbox and will use the strategies in this book when needed. We also hope you have learned that we are all sensory beings, and we all function differently. Since our brains are all different, and each of our bodies perceive sensory information in a unique way, it is important to understand not only your child's sensory profile, but your own, as well. The better you understand yourself, the better you can understand your children, your friends, and the rest of your family.

We try to bring you a neutral voice, through our research and personal experiences. We know that not everything we talk about will work for every child, but we hope you got something out of the information presented in this book and that you can take away a feeling of relief from knowing how to help your child be healthy and happy.

SENSORY PARENTING: THE ELEMENTARY YEARS

Sensory-Friendly Meals and Special Diets

What is a food allergy versus a food sensitivity? According to the National Institute of Allergy and Infectious Diseases, a food allergy is an "adverse immune response that occurs reproducibly on exposure to a given food and is distinct from other adverse responses to food, such as food intolerances, pharmacologic reactions, and toxin-mediated reactions."[24]

If you are allergic to a specific food, you may exhibit symptoms like hives, wheezing, difficulty breathing, swelling of the lips and throat, and developing a skin rash.

A food intolerance is the inability to digest a food. A food sensitivity is a less specific sensitivity that may be mediated by the release of the antibody "immunoglobulin G," which can produce gastrointestinal and nongastrointestinal reactions (such as nasal congestion, chronic sinusitis, recurrent ear infections, fatigue, asthma, heart burn, diarrhea or constipation, and eczema).[25] Immunoglobulin G is released by the body as a gradual response to a food, with subtle symptoms occurring 12 to 24 hours or more after ingestion that may be long term in nature.

If you are lactose intolerant, you actually have an imbalance between the amount of ingested lactose (sugar) in your body and your capacity to break down the lactose. The clinical symptoms of lactose intolerance may show up as abdominal pain, diarrhea, nausea, flatulence, and/or bloating. Young children are not lactose intolerant, unless they have a metabolic disorder or a disease that affects the top of the villi (fingerlike projections that line the intestinal walls) in the gut. Lactose intolerance is a disease of aging enzymes. It is more likely that a child will have a sensitivity to cow's milk protein, rather than lactose intolerance.

Food and Your Child's Mood

Neurotransmitters (brain chemicals that affect how we think and feel) are composed of the building blocks of protein and choline obtained from our diet.[26] Anger, anxiety, depression, fatigue, impulsiveness, and distractible disorders are all being linked to food intake and nutritional deficiencies. You want to ensure that your child has the proper nutrition for her brain to continue to be wired, develop, and thrive, as well as fostering her physical and even emotional development. Elizabeth Somer, MS, RD, author of *Food & Mood*, explains that you're building your child's food associations and memories, as well as the emotional cues that urge her to eat and to crave certain foods. This in turn shapes her food preferences.[27] While this may seem like a lot of pressure and difficult to figure out in the current climate of massive marketing campaigns, the easiest way to figure out what is good to feed your child is by monitoring her moods, behavior, mental clarity, and ability to function after eating. Feed her the foods that work for her body and yours.

What to Feed Your Growing Child

If you're concerned that there may be a connection between your child's ailments and food, a wonderful resource is *What's Eating Your Child*, by Kelly Dorman, MS, LND. Kelly explores anxiety, ear infections, stomachaches, picky eating, rashes, ADHD, and more, as well as what every parent can do about it.

As a girl who was raised in a farming community, I used to think that organic food was a bunch of marketing nonsense, but as more and more research has come out about the health benefits of organic produce, I've converted to the organic side. With organic fruits and vegetables, there are still some pesticides and fertilizers, but the fruits and vegetables are not genetically modified. Often, organic fruits and vegetables are more expensive, but more and more grocery chains are becoming organic friendly and also more competitive, since consumers are wising up and making healthier choices for their families. We get enough food additives and chemicals from everyday foods and products, so why not limit the toxic intake with our most nutrition-rich resources? Organic fruits and vegetables may not look as healthy as genetically modified fruits and vegetables, because there are no red dyes in the tomatoes or growth hormones added to the broccoli.

If you shop in bulk at stores such as Costco, which I do often, you can find brands of fruits and vegetables that haven't been pumped with chemicals. Also, washing your produce after getting home can remove some of the harmful pesticides. If you're shopping for canned food, check for additional sugars, such as fructose or corn syrup, as well as additives and preservatives.

Kids and Protein

Protein is the primary source of nutrients for the creation of neurotransmitters in the brain. That being the case, we highly recommended that you talk to your pediatrician and/or registered dietitian or pediatric nutritionist to ensure that your child is receiving the proper amounts of protein each day. As there is no one-size-fits-all dietary plan, you need to research the best sources of protein for your child, taking into account any food sensitivities, allergies, or intolerances. While some kids do well with meat, others respond better to peanut butter or cheese.

Kids and Salt

What is salt? It's sodium and chloride. Sometimes, we crave salty foods, like potato chips or ham, and this could mean that we are dehydrated, as salt makes us want to drink water and other fluids. Other times, salt causes us to bloat and hold onto liquids. Salt is in almost every processed food out there, including those pancakes you ate for breakfast, the bread and the soup you ate at lunch, and the meatloaf and mashed potatoes you had for dinner. Get the picture? We eat a lot of salt without thinking about it. Watch how much extra salt you sprinkle on your meal.

Kids and Sugar

Consuming sugar, or glucose, is known to lead to bursts of energy, rapid mood swings, hunger, irritability, and physical weakness.[26] Be wary of junk foods, treats, cereals, and products that may cause your child to have an overload of glucose, which will in turn mess with his natural insulin production and distribution.

More often than not, you and your child are going to eat some sugar throughout your day, because it is in most foods; however, try to keep it to a minimum and be aware of how much you are consuming. While sugar is tasty, it's not necessarily good for a child's growing brain or his waistline. A cookie here and there will not hurt him, unless he doesn't feel good afterward or he has an adverse reaction to the cupcake he ate after lunch.

The different names of sugar on labels include sugar, brown sugar, glucose, fructose, lactose, maltose, sucrose, corn syrup, high-fructose corn syrup, and maltodextrin, amongst others.

How to introduce new foods to your sensory-sensitive child:

- Give him a preferred food first, or something that is crunchy
- Make a food book with your child to help motivate him. Pick out pictures of foods your child likes and what he likes about that food. Try things that may have a similar texture or taste.
- Engage in food play. This can be tricky as your child gets older, as you don't want him to make a mess of every meal. What we suggest is that you let him feel the food with his fingers, pick it up, and may-be experiment a little—especially if it's something you know he's not going to ingest. Let him become more familiar with it, and hopefully it will make it into his mouth at some point.
- Have your child assist in making the food. Cooking and baking are great ways for children to become more interested in the food they're eating. Have them stir, add spices, and try any part of the food preparation to engage them.

SENSORY PARENTING: THE ELEMENTARY YEARS

Pets

Some of you may have had your animals for a number of years before having children, and, as you've found out, having animals and kids together can be an adjustment. We have learned that a lot of things you may have been oblivious to before will grate on your nerves and senses. Here are some tips on helping "Fido" and your child's world merge and some things to factor in if you're considering adding to your urban farm.

Two things are a guarantee: Your animal will eat, and your animal will poop. In any local pet store, you can seek out a food that is tasty for your pet, while the smell of it won't make you nauseous. There are foods to help your pet's digestion, for a reduction in poop production—but there will always be poop: regular stools and diarrhea, and perhaps even vomiting. Most likely, the one staying home with the children is the one who gets to clean this mess up, so invest in some gloves and plastic bags. That Diaper Champ can be used for animal poop, too! I've found that putting baking powder into the bottom of your trash can helps keep odors under control, as well. You will have to dump your trash daily if there is any poop in it. Do not let this sit in your kitchen or laundry room overnight, emitting toxins into the air in your home.

We recommend cleaning up all indoor animal-related accidents with nontoxic cleaning products. This way, you protect your senses and your animal's senses, as well as your child's senses.

Birds

Beautiful birds with their pretty, colorful feathers are usually pretty noisy. They squawk, tweet, and chirp, and some even talk. They can rattle their cages and enjoy a whistle or bell from time to time. Birds are not for the auditory sensitive.

Cats

Felines are known for their independence, which can make for a great pet if you're gone at work all day. The cons are that they are also known for their dander, stinky cat box, fur balls, clawing, and scratching. Good news ladies, you get to pass over cat-box cleaning duties while pregnant and nursing to keep you and your baby safe from the risk of acquiring toxoplasmosis (a parasitic infection that can be transmitted through contact with a cat's fecal matter). Many children are allergic to cat dander, so watch your child for signs of a runny nose, irritated eyes, or dark circles under the eyes. These mostly nocturnal animals may also keep your family awake if they're constantly playing throughout the night. You need your sleep, and so does your child. Maybe kitty can sleep in the garage. Smelly litter boxes are not recommended for the olfactory (nose) sensitive. The litter box can be moved to the garage, and you'll have to make sure you clean it out frequently to decrease the smell. The trade-off is that the soft tactile input and companionship you'll get in return is very rewarding for both kids and adults, as is the bond your child will form with your pet.

> **OT Tip:**
> Animals are so good for kids, especially for those with sensory difficulties. They read people's cues and can sense when a child is in distress. I have seen both dogs and cats help calm people down when they were upset.

Dogs

Oh how we love our dogs! This favorite pet is often forgiven for its dander, the hair it sheds everywhere, its incessant barking, and its rambunctious and playful demeanor because of its unwavering loyalty and love. Dogs dote on their owners, and how can you not love that? However, dogs aren't for everyone, and they can be a sensory challenge. Their dander can be potent and tough on a family member with allergies. They're often unaware of their size and can knock over your child. Parents are oddly oblivious to the strong jaws and teeth of their dogs, thinking that their cute and cuddly companion wouldn't hurt anyone. Once the dog encounters a toddler holding a ham sandwich, however, all bets are off. Some dogs can become jealous of a new baby, and others are oblivious to anything other than their food bowl. There are many resources to help you with your dog if you're having behavioral problems while you introduce a baby into the mix. We suggest getting these under control as quickly as possible so that your child and dog(s) may have a healthy and solid relationship as they grow up.

A common mistake that people make is bringing home a guard dog for their family and then expecting the stay-at-home mom to walk the dog and the baby in the stroller. This can be a disaster if Mom cannot handle the dog and if the dog is extremely territorial and protective of the baby. Be sure to research the different breeds to find a suitable dog for you and your family. You can always get a terrier and invest in an alarm system.

If you're thinking of buying a cute little miniature dog to put sweaters on, be sure to research how yappy your little prince could be. Keep all of your family members' auditory sensitivities in mind before purchasing a 24-hour barking toy. There's usually a pretty strict no-return policy.

Service dogs can be extremely helpful for those who have sensory issues. They're most commonly used with the blind. They're amazing for veterans returning from war who need help with traumatic flash-backs and disorientation, and they're now commonly used to aid children with autism. Look into your local service-dog agencies if you think that having one of these dogs would be helpful to your family. Or, see if they've got any dogs that didn't pass their rigorous tests! They'll be highly trained, and maybe they just can't see as well or they have one shorter leg. There is a difference between service dog, therapy dog/pet, and companion dog/pet. Make sure you address your family's needs if you are acquiring one of these types of animals.

Ferrets

Ferrets can sometimes run free in a house and are treated somewhat like cats and dogs. Just follow sanitary guidelines on cleaning up after your ferret(s), and, as a precautionary measure, keep it out of your child's room. You will have to train your ferret to use the litter box and do what is called "nip-training," so your ferret doesn't take a bite out of your youngster.

Fish

A word to the wise—goldfish die, sometimes before you even get them home. As someone who has had a "magic" spotted goldfish for 5 years (who periodically makes a trip to the pet store for a cleaning), do not bring home a fish in "The Little Mermaid" aquarium unless you're ready to talk to your little one about life and death. If you're going more for the family aquarium, with either salt water or fresh water—fantastic.

> **OT Tip:**
> Fish are known to be mesmerizing and soothing. Hospitals and doctors' and dentists' offices use fish tanks to help soothe their patients in the waiting room. This can be very helpful for a kid with overwhelming sensory issues, who may have difficulty self-soothing.

After watching "Finding Nemo," your child will be even more thrilled about having a fish for a pet. Just make sure your child doesn't bang on the glass with her hand or a toy, in case the glass breaks or falls on her. Always take precautionary safety measures.

Know that fish can be a lot of work. You have to clean their tanks often, and maintaining the proper amount of algae can be a science experiment in itself. If you don't like getting your hands wet, this isn't the pet for you.

Gerbils, Hamsters, and Guinea Pigs

These nocturnal rodents are a little kid's favorite. They're small, cute, and pretty active, and they enjoy burrowing, which makes them fun to watch. Take note that a hamster plus a wheel equals an all-night running party. If you bring home a boy and a girl hamster, be ready for a million babies, as hamsters multiply as fast as "Gremlins." That, or they will sometimes fight to the death and kill each other, which can make for an interesting scene with a screaming child. Make sure to keep the hamster cage in a place where you will most likely find an unsightly crime scene first, before your child does.

You might find guinea pigs adorable, unless you've had one squeak all night in your bedroom. I'm not exaggerating when I say they squeak *all night*, and they're quite loud. They're also not particularly friendly (think bunny rabbit), and they have pretty big teeth (again, think bunny rabbit). However, many kids in 4-H adore them and enjoy taking care of them until the time of their local fair.

Bunny Rabbits

While rabbits are adorable creatures, they're not commonly great house pets. An important factor is that rabbits are nervous and typically don't enjoy being held. They will shake with fright, kick, bite, and struggle to be released. This fragile animal is also quick and can be hard to catch. It's amazing how good they are at hiding. Think again if you are looking for a pet your child can cuddle with.

Rats

The best-kept secret is that rats make wonderful pets for children. They're easily tamed and become attached to their owner, taking on their owner's temperament at times. They're pretty low maintenance but like to exercise and play. Some owners swear their rat comes when called by name. Rats are intelligent, as well, with males being notably lazier than the females. With a life span of 2 to 3 years, the commitment is pretty short-lived for these nocturnal love bugs. Who knew?

Reptiles

Reptiles are for the more mature pet owner. They're relatively easy to care for, if you can stomach feeding them live crickets (who will chirp loudly until eaten) and/or mice (who will squeak loudly until eaten). They usually require a sun lamp to keep them warm, regardless of the temperature in your home, so if you're light sensitive, these may not be good pets for you.

While geckoes and some breeds of lizards are relatively harmless, I can't think of anything more frightening than finding a snake slithering up against my sleeping child. Know your state's safety guidelines for owning reptiles and take extra precautionary measures. Or, play it extra safe and wait till your child is in high school before starting your cobra farm.

Turtles, both water and land varieties, are interesting pets, but again, they require a lot of care. Water turtles are susceptible to disease, so make sure your child washes his hands directly after handling the turtle. Also, water turtles scratch on the glass walls of their aquariums while swimming, which can be annoying to sensitive ears. Desert tortoises hibernate from November to around March, making them a perfect half-a-year pet. (The best part—you don't have to worry about securing a pet sitter during your winter holiday!). Turtles are also yummy snacks for crows and other flying predators, however, so be wary if they're kept outside during the summer months. Most reptiles will not hold your child's attention for very long, as they're not the most exciting creatures for a child to watch.

Outdoor Animals

If you are fortunate enough to have outdoor animals and livestock, such as cows, sheep, pigs, horses, chickens, and turkeys, just take note of your child's allergies and whether he has an aversion to an animal's dander or poop. Chickens and turkeys are messy birds, so clean their coops often, and make sure you wash your baby's hands if he's helped you gather eggs. If you take the proper precautionary actions to ensure that your animals and children are safe, you will most likely avoid any sensory issues with your kids living in a farm environment. Now, if you can only get that rooster to crow later in the morning!

SENSORY PARENTING: THE ELEMENTARY YEARS

A Parent's Role in Play

You do not have to play with your child every second of every day, and you also don't want to play with your child only once a week. Moderation is key and allowing her to learn to play by herself is important, too. Embrace what your child is interested in and what she gravitates toward.

Don't be the pushy parent who always expects her child to be the best. Whether he wins or loses is okay, as long as he tries his best. Find your child's strengths and help him to excel in a particular area if that is important to you, but don't resort to name-calling or ridicule, such as "Don't be a scaredy-cat" or "When I was your age, I could score 10 goals a game!" Sarcasm and what you might consider light-hearted joking can be belittling for a child. Many children already feel powerless and judged throughout the day, whether it be at day care or preschool or with their older siblings or cousins. Empower your child so that he may excel in the future.

Play can be emotional for both you and your child. Examine and learn to control emotions through play. For example, make a tent and be scared with your child as you pretend you're camping in the desert and hear coyotes howling. Be sad with your child while pretending that you didn't get to go to a birthday party. You can be "pretend angry" with your child, too, but with all these pretend games, make sure your child knows that you are playing and not really mad at him. These exercises help your child to learn how to calm himself down while he's feeling these emotions and also to learn how to react in these situations. Show him how to switch emotional gears. Be sad, then happy, then frightened, then sad in a matter of moments. Always finish with laughter and find a peaceful center. This will help your child relieve stress and pent-up emotions and learn that it is okay to feel negative emotions and that there are ways to control them.

Funsucker

If there is one thing you not want to be known as to your friends, it is a "funsucker"—someone who takes the fun out of any and every situation. Life isn't perfect, so don't try to force it to be or try to make your kids perfect. Let them make mistakes, even in play. Don't turn every moment into a photo opportunity. Snap your shots at a designated area or time and then get on with your day, or take a million photos during the day and only keep the good ones. Take silly shots on your digital camera, too, and show your child—she'll think outrageous photos of herself are hilarious!

Roughhousing

Wrestling and roughhousing are a normal part of development. Both boys and girls will enjoy a good rough and tumble with Daddy, usually right before bedtime—exactly when you DON'T want them to get riled up. According to Dr Lawrence J. Cohen, author of *Playful Parenting*, wrestling helps children test their physical strength, control their anger, and learn physical boundaries.[28] Many children will experiment with wrestling, hitting, and pulling before trying out their skills on their peers in rough play.

Keep your rough play sessions short and stop immediately if anyone gets hurt. Let your child know it's not okay to hurt Daddy, either—he can assert himself but needs to learn how to control himself. Make sure he understands that there is no biting, hair-pulling, or foul play in wrestle time. It's more of a proprioceptive exercise, if you will, by providing just the right level of resistance for both you and the child.

Pay close attention to whether your child is getting too aggressive or out of control. If he is, stop immediately. Tickling is not allowed in roughhousing play, as it evokes the feeling of being out of control, which is the opposite lesson you are teaching during roughhouse play.

It's a good idea to cuddle afterward, to keep your parent-child connection strong and to let your child know that you are both okay. Snuggle together on the couch while watching a DVD or reading a book together. Always end on a positive note.

Important things to remember as an adult:

- Play with your child often, especially when he is young.
- Teach him that play is a vital skill in life.
- Create playful atmospheres, and when the opportunity to play presents itself, get down on the floor and interact with your child.
- Don't be rigid—be flexible.
- Don't be afraid to be silly. Use props and pretend items are something they are not (pick up the banana and pretend Grandpa is calling on the phone).
- Understand that play changes in a child's eyes. Learn to go with whatever your child is into during each stage of his development.

SENSORY PARENTING: THE ELEMENTARY YEARS

Coexisting Conditions

Does My Child Have Autism?

The world of autism is confusing and complicated for parents to comprehend. It covers such a massive umbrella of diagnoses within the one label of autism: pervasive developmental disorder not otherwise specified, Asperger syndrome, low-, mild-, and high-functioning autism—I've even heard the term "autistic-like." While the trend was and may still be securing a diagnosis of autism to be able to receive services for your child, the state and local government systems, school systems, and private practices are now so flooded that the autism label is no longer a magic pass into regional centers (state-run centers that offer services and resources for children with disabilities), early-intervention programs, insurance carriers, and school districts. Many children are now being described as "recovered," and some camps argue that those children didn't really have autism—perhaps they had sensory dysfunction and nutritional deficiencies. Other groups consider these children to be spoiled brats or difficult as a result of bad parenting, and some believe that those with severe autism have cognitive impairment.

There have been major breakthroughs in autism awareness with movies like "Autism: The Musical," and Temple Grandin's life story, which aired on HBO; however, people are still unsure how to specifically define autism and, once diagnosed, how to go about treating and/or living with autism. As a new parent, you might be fearful that your child will catch autism, like the flu, or maybe you feel autism couldn't happen to you and your family. Following are some questions to ask yourself if you're exploring the possibility that autism is affecting your child.

Do you feel like something is "wrong?" Do you feel that your child is not like other children and doesn't fit in? Are you having a difficult time understanding what your child wants and needs? Do you want to burn all the books that aren't giving you the guidance you need because your child doesn't fit into the category they're talking about? Have you become overprotective of your child's behaviors? Do you make up excuses as to why your child is not developing at the same rate as other children?

Being that autism is on the rise and receiving media attention, more and more parents have the privilege of securing a diagnosis for their babies and toddlers and receiving early-intervention treatments. If you have any concerns, do not feel embarrassed or paranoid—have your child evaluated. If it turns out that your child does not have autism, and you feel silly for pushing for the tests, then congratulations! But if your child does have autism, early intervention can help, and the sooner you start getting the appropriate treatment for your child, the better.

Possible Signs of Autism

My child:
- Lines up toys
- Is unable to tolerate someone else playing with his toys or changing what he is doing
- Has difficulty transitioning
- Exhibits decreased eye contact
- Exhibits decreased language skills, has difficulty communicating (has few or no verbal skills)
- Is constantly repeating words or short groups of words or memorizing and repeating entire TV shows

- Cries and throws tantrums for no reason
- Shows little or no emotional connection with others
- Is unable to pretend-play
- Performs repeated body movements ("stimming," such as hand or arm flapping, rocking, hitting himself over and over again)
- Is a picky eater
- Has difficulty sleeping or transitioning from being awake to going to sleep
- Is fearful of people in general (at parks and family functions, in public, and at home)
- Is fearless (is completely unaware of any safety concerns or danger)
- Is overly fascinated and obsessed with one item or subject for an extended period

If your child exhibits several of these signs, you are probably okay. But if your child demonstrates more than a few of these behaviors, it's worth talking to your pediatrician about it.

Mom Tip:
There is a helpful checklist, M-CHAT, compiled by Diana Robins, Deborah Fein, and Marianne Barton, that is available online if you'd like to print a copy, fill it out, and take it in to your pediatric physician as a starting point when discussing concerns you have about your child.

Does My Child Have ADHD?

Attention-deficit/hyperactivity disorder, or ADHD, is another term that you might not have heard of before you had a baby, but you've likely been hearing all the buzz about it now. Like autism, ADHD has different levels and subtypes and a variety of treatments. Most are quick to medicate for this disorder, which can be positive for some kids and negative for others. Again, as a mother, I advise you to educate yourself and explore your options and various treatments for your child. Find out all the pros and cons of each medication, and talk to other parents with children who take these medications. What are the adverse health risks? What kind of reaction can you expect? What should you be looking for and monitoring?

I'm a big believer in searching for the underlying cause of any and all medical conditions. Can it be improved with diet and nutrition? Are there behavioral modifications and treatments you can try? Would sensory-integration therapy be effective? Or perhaps a combination of all of the above? Work with your developmental pediatrician and seek out a specialist who specifically treats children with ADHD.

Be an advocate for your child and make sure he's treated with respect in the school system. Even though he may be more difficult for the teacher to handle, he deserves a positive learning environment.

Signs of ADHD

My child:

- Is hyperactive
- Is impulsive
- Has an inability to attend to a task, even for a few minutes
- Does not appear to hear you when you call his name or talk to him
- Has difficulty organizing tasks
- Often loses things (toys, school assignments, etc)
- Is easily distracted and has difficulty getting refocused on the task

Symptoms must be present for at least 6 months to warrant a diagnosis, and the symptoms must be observable in two or more settings. Some symptoms must be present before age 7, and they must be severe enough to cause significant difficulties with performing functional life skills.

Cerebral Palsy

Cerebral palsy is the inability to control motor function. It manifests as decreased coordination abilities and is usually diagnosed within the first 6 months of life. It is sometimes diagnosed at birth. Cerebral palsy can range from very mild to severe. As a therapist, I have seen children with a diagnosis of cerebral palsy, and you cannot even tell. They may have slightly decreased coordination on one side and wear a foot brace, or have one hand that is slightly weaker than the other. They could also have a typically developing brain and cognitive level, but their physical body is delayed. Some children with cerebral palsy are in wheelchairs. In more severe cases, a child may not be able to take care of herself and is completely dependent on a caretaker.

Children with cerebral palsy benefit from multiple types of therapy, depending on their needs, which include occupational therapy, physical therapy, and speech therapy. Physical therapists can help them with walking, leg strength, balance, fitting orthotics for their feet and ankles, if needed, and wheelchair fitting. OTs will work on play skills, developmental milestones, core strengthening, self-feeding, dressing, grooming, writing or using adaptive communication devices, and more. Speech-language pathologists work on language development, understanding of language, feeding skills, communication devices, and more. If your child has been diagnosed with cerebral palsy, you need to research the diagnosis and possible therapies and treatments that can be helpful to your child. After assigning a diagnosis, most doctors will help set you up with the correct resources.

> **OT Tip:**
> Always remember that when conducting research on the Internet, make sure the Web sites you view are valid and written by physicians and experts. Take information that you get from the Internet with a grain of salt and know that every child is different, so just because one mom's blog says that her child needs one thing, this does not necessarily mean it will fit the needs of your child.

Hypotonia

Hypotonia is decreased muscle tone and can be caused by trauma, genetics, and central nervous system disorders such as cerebral palsy, Down syndrome, and muscular dystrophy. Usually the cause is unknown. Babies with hypotonia are typically called "floppy babies" because they have poor muscle tone, and their limbs tend to be loose and floppy. Usually muscle weakness occurs because of poor muscle tone, necessitating physical and occupational therapy to help increase muscular strength. Children with hypotonia can have difficulty eating and swallowing and require specific occupational therapy or speech-language pathology treatment, as these difficulties can be a safety risk because of choking and/or aspiration. (Aspiration is when food enters the airway after swallowing.)

Cognitive Impairment

Cognitive impairment (previously known as mental retardation) is the most common of developmental disabilities.[29] For a child to receive a diagnosis of cognitive impairment, she has to be tested by a developmental pediatrician or a psychologist in various areas, such as intelligence (IQ) testing, adaptive skills, and developmental living skills. Cognitive impairment can vary from severe to mild, or even borderline. Children with mild cognitive impairment tend to have IQs between 55 and 70. These children are still able to live full lives, marry, hold down jobs, and interact socially with their peers. Children with moderate cognitive impairment tend to have IQ scores between 40 and 55. They require more assistance to function in their everyday lives and have more difficulty interacting within society. Children with severe cognitive impairment have IQ scores between 25 and 40 and require extensive support but can usually learn some way to communicate.[29]

Many times, cognitive impairment can coexist with other disabilities, like Down syndrome, autism, and genetic disorders. Other times, a child can have increased cognitive abilities but have other delays.

Seizures

Seizure disorders can range from infantile seizures to epilepsy. "A seizure may be defined as a temporary, involuntary change of consciousness, behavior, motor activity, sensation, or automatic functioning."[29] Individuals are considered to have epilepsy if they have recurring seizures.[29] Seizures can be a scary thing, especially if you have never seen or experienced someone having a seizure episode. If your child is having what is called a generalized tonic-clonic seizure (grand mal), she may fall to the ground, stop breathing, or experience a loss of consciousness, a loss of bowel and bladder control, and contracting or convulsing muscles. If your child is having an absence seizure (petit mal), she may show signs of loss of consciousness, but this could be so brief that you don't even catch it. Children who have this type of seizure usually stay in one position and look as if they are staring off into space. They may also blink rapidly. Infantile spasms typically begin at 6 months and disappear around 24 months, but they can be detrimental to a child's development, since this is a crucial age of motor and cognitive development.

There is that old saying, "Laughter is the best medicine," and we believe that to be true. As someone who works in the hospital environment, I know that all children, no matter how sick they are, enjoy a good laugh (make sure it's not painful for them!) or a nice smile.

References

1. Ahn RR, Miller LJ, Milberger S, McIntosh DN. Prevalence of parents' perceptions of sensory processing: disorders among kindergarten children. *Am J Occup Ther.* 2004;58:287-293.

2. Ben-Sasson A, Carter AS, Briggs-Gowan MJ. Sensory over-responsivity in elementary school: prevalence and social-emotional correlates. *J Abnorm Child Psychol.* 2009;37:705-716.

3. Hoopes A, Appelbaum S. *Eye Power: A Cutting Edge Report on Vision Therapy.* BookSurge Publishing; 2009:18-19.

4. Madaule P. *When Listening Comes Alive: A Guide to Effective Learning and Communication.* Norval, Ontario, Canada: Moulin Publishing; 1994:114.

5. Gilbert A. *What the Nose Knows: The Science of Scent in Everyday Life.* New York, NY: Crown Publishing Group; 2008:29, 48, 93.

6. Miller LJ, Anzalone M, Lane S, Cermak SA, Osten E. Concept evolution in sensory integration: a proposed nosology for diagnosis. *Am J Occup Ther.* 2007;61:135–140.

7. Bailer DS, Miller LJ. *No Longer A SECRET: Unique Common Sense Strategies for Children with Sensory or Motor Challenges.* Arlington, TX: Sensory World; 2011:151-162.

8. Eisenberg N, Hofer C, Vaughan J. Effortful control and its socioeconomical consequences. In: Gross JJ, ed. *Handbook of Emotion Regulation.* New York, NY: Guilford Press; 2007:287-306.

9. Greenspan S, Degangi G, Wieder S. *The Functional Emotional Assessment Scale (FEAS) for Infancy and Early Childhood.* Bethesda, MD: Interdisciplinary Counsel on Development and Learning Disorders; 2001: xi-xiv, 3-53.

10. Lewit EM, Baker LS. School readiness. *Future Child.* 1995;5(2):128-139.

11. Lavoie R. *It's So Much Work to Be Your Friend.* New York, NY: Touchstone; 2005:22.

12. Siegel DJ, Bryson TP. *The Whole-Brain Child.* New York, NY: DelaCorte Press; 2011:126, 129.

13. Mayer DP. *Overcoming School Anxiety.* New York, NY: Amacom; 2008:188.

14. Siegel DJ, Bryson TP. *The Whole-Brain Child.* New York, NY: DelaCorte Press; 2011:28, 29.

15. Attwood T. *Exploring Feelings: Cognitive Behaviour Therapy to Manage Anxiety.* Arlington, TX: Future Horizons; 2004:3.

16. McGonigal J. *Reality Is Broken: Why Games Make Us Better and How they Can Change the World.* New York, NY: The Penguin Press; 2011:4, 11, 21, 25.

17. Taylor J. *Learn to Have Fun with Your Senses.* Arlington, TX: Sensory World; 2011:63-66.

18. Fountain H. Suppressing tinnitus with music therapy. *New York Times.* January 5, 2010:1

19. King B. *Music Therapy: Another Path to Learning and Communication for Children on the Autism Spectrum.* Arlington, TX: Future Horizons; 2004:12, 16.

20. Service Animal. Wikipedia. *http://en.wikipedia.org/wiki/Service_animal*. Accessed April 26, 2012.

21. Tomcheck SD, Dunn W. Sensory processing in children with and without autism: a comparative study using the Short Sensory Profile. *Am J Occup Ther.* 2007;61:190-200.

22. Sicile-Kara C. What is sensory processing disorder and how is it related to autism? *Psychology Today.* March 2, 2010:1.

23. Miller LJ, Nielsen DM, Schoen SA. Attention-deficit hyperactivity disorder and sensory modulation disorder: a comparison of behavior and physiology. *Res Dev Disabilities. 2012*;33:804-818.

24. Food allergy. National Institute of Allergy and Infectious Diseases. *www.niaid.nih.gov/topics/foodallergy/Pages/default.aspx*. Accessed May 15, 2012.

25. Sierpina VS. *The Healthy Gut Workbook: Whole-Body Healing for Heartburn, Ulcers, Constipation, IBS, Diverticulosis, & More.* Oakland, CA: New Harbinger Publications.

26. Challem J. *The Food-Mood Solution.* Hoboken, NJ: John Wiley & Sons; 2007:4; 52.

27. Somer E. *Food & Mood: The Complete Guide to Eating Well and Feeling Your Best.* New York, NY: Holt Paperbacks; 1999: 61.

28. Cohen LJ. *Playful Parenting: A Bold New Way to Nurture Close Connections, Solve Behavior Problems, and Encourage Children's Confidence.* New York, NY: Ballantine; 2001:93-112.

29. Case-Smith J. *Occupational Therapy for Children.* 4th ed. St Louis, MO: Mosby; 2001:85-87, 155-156, 163-164, 528-535.

SENSORY PARENTING: THE ELEMENTARY YEARS

Resources

Here are some online sensory resources that we love:

Making Sense of Sensory Processing Disorder
makingsenseofspd.com

> Teresa Denny, the mother of a child with SPD, writes this blog about "practical tips to make sensory challenges a little easier."

Pedia Staff Newsletter
pediastaff.com/pedia-receive-our-newsletter

> This comprehensive resource is all about special needs and pediatrics. The newsletter has the most interesting and informative articles, and it's updated every Friday. It's a must read.

sensoryflow.com

> This site has excellent resources that are organized into an easily accessible format. You'll find videos, articles, and blogs. Cat Lichtenbelt is a master at keeping us up to date on all things sensory.

sensoryfun.com

> Bonnie Arnwine, author of *Starting Sensory Therapy*, has a Web site of resources, as well as a blog. And it is fun!

sensory-processing-disorder.com

> This site was created by an OT named Michelle, who has a daughter with SPD. It is a wonderful resource, with articles and examples of activities to try with your child. It's kept up to date with the latest research.

sensorysmarts.com

On this site, the amazing Lindsey Biel, MA, OTR/L, provides articles, resources, and tips about living with SPD. Her expertise and advice are a treasure, making this a "go to" spot for us. She coauthored the award-winning book *Raising a Sensory Smart Child.*

sensorysupport.org

This site was founded by Meg Schecter to provide a hub for families of children with SPD. You'll find other parents to connect with, as well as the latest articles and research.

sensoryworld.org

You or your child can create online sensory rooms on this site. These can be very soothing and creative. It's great for adults with learning disabilities to do, as well.

specialhappens.com

This site was created by Gina St Aubin, for parents of children with special needs. She encourages us to discover, embrace, educate, advocate, treasure, and laugh. It's inspiring!

SPD Blogger Network
www.spdbloggernetwork.com

This network was founded by Hartley Steiner, the award-winning author of the books *This Is Gabriel Making Sense of School* and *Sensational Journeys.* This network has many contributing bloggers. Sign up for the newsletter, so you can automatically receive the top five articles of the month!

SPD Foundation
spdfoundation.net

Founded by Dr Lucy Miller, this Web site is an SPD resource like no other. Learn about the latest research and find an OT trained in sensory integration near you.

Training Happy Hearts

traininghappyhearts.blogspot.com

> This blog is written by Martianne, a mom of three, who home-schools her kids and shares her sensory experiences. It is very creative and has many adventurous ways to incorporate sensory activities into your child's life.

understandingSPD.com

> Angie Voss, OTR/L, specializes in OT with a sensory-integration approach and has a plethora of resources and articles available. She offers free PDF downloads that are extremely helpful. Angie is also the author of *Understanding Your Child's Sensory Signals* and *Your Essential Guide to Understanding Sensory Processing Disorder.*

Here are some printed resources we recommend:

Building Bridges Through Sensory Integration, by Ellen Yack, Paula Aquilla, and Shirley Sutton

Growing an In-Sync Child, by Carol Kranowitz and Joye Newman

Raising a Sensory Smart Child, by Lindsey Biel and Nancy Peske

Sensational Kids: Hope and Help for Children with Sensory Processing Disorder, by Lucy Jane Miller and Doris A. Fuller

Parenting a Child with Sensory Processing Disorder, by Christopher R. Auer and Susan L. Blumberg

Starting Sensory Therapy: Fun Activities for the Home and Classroom! by Bonnie Arnwine

No Longer A Secret: Unique Common Sense Strategies for Children with Sensory or Motor Challenges, by Doreit Bialer and Lucy J. Miller

S.I. Focus magazine: A subscription to *S.I. Focus* includes quarterly digital magazines, packed with articles and top-notch information from the experts. It's a must-read for professionals and parents alike. For a free preview, go to *SIFocus.com*.

INDEX

Note: an *f* after a page number indicates a figure.

A

M

N

O

R

S

Y

About the Authors

Britt Collins, MS, OTR, graduated from Colorado State University with a master's degree in occupational therapy and has practiced in a variety of settings, including sensory-integration clinics, schools, homes, and pediatric hospitals. **Jackie Linder Olson** is a producer and writer whose son has Sensory Processing Disorder.

Britt Collins, MS, OTR

Jackie and Britt created an occupational-therapy DVD series for parents, caregivers, and educators, to visually learn the basics of occupational therapy and how to implement it into a child's daily life. The DVDs include "OT in the Home," "OT in the School," "OT for Children with Autism, Special Needs and Typical," and "Yoga for Children with Special Needs."

The duo cofounded Special Needs United, with the goals of bringing occupational therapy to families of children with special needs. Britt currently resides in Denver, Colorado, and works at the STAR Center

Jackie Linder Olson

with Dr Lucy J. Miller. Jackie resides in Los Angeles, California. Both can be found touring the country, speaking about the benefits of occupational therapy for children.

SENSORY PARENTING: THE ELEMENTARY YEARS

Also by Britt Collins and Jackie Linder Olson

www.sensoryworld.com